Hank Williams, *So Lonesome*

Hank Williams,
So Lonesome

BILL KOON

UNIVERSITY PRESS OF MISSISSIPPI • JACKSON

www.upress.state.ms.us

Hank Williams: A Bio-Bibliography, by George W. Koon, was
originally published in hard cover by Greenwood Press, Westport, CT,
1983. Copyright © 1983 by George W. Koon. This edition by arrangement
with Greenwood Publishing Group, Inc. All rights reserved.

09 08 07 06 05 04 03 02 01   4 3 2 1

∞

Library of Congress Cataloging-in-Publication Data

Koon, George William.
[Hank Williams]
Hank Williams, so lonesome / Bill Koon.
p.   cm. — (American made music series)
Originally published: Hank Williams. Westport, Conn.: Greenwood Press, 1983.
Includes bibliographical references (p.   ) and index.
Discography: p.
ISBN 1-57806-283-7 (pbk.: alk. paper)
1. Williams, Hank, 1923–1953.   2. Country musicians—United States—
Biography.   I. Series.
ML420.W55 K7 2002
782.421642'092—dc21
[B]
2001025866

British Library Cataloging-in-Publication Data available

FOR GABRIELE AND MATTEA

CONTENTS

PREFACE

Fifty years ago, my father took our family from Columbia, South Carolina to Nashville to see The Grand Ole Opry. My memory of the show is vague. I recall the things of childhood: the R.C. Colas the square dancers drank on stage, a master of ceremonies who actually solicited applause from the audience, and my souvenir Ernest Tubb songbook. Looking back now, I realize that Hank Williams might have performed that night. I knew his songs, and I had a playmate nicknamed "Bocephus," but I did not really know who Hank was. I may have seen him, though, and I expect to tell my grandchildren that, indeed, I once saw country music's greatest star.

A small town near where I live now features a large feed and seed store. It is a Quonset, probably of World War II vintage, its roof curving nearly to the ground. Before the feed and seed, before television, the building had been a movie house. Several of my older friends in the area have told me that once Hank Williams dropped by to give a free performance there. Another rumor among them is that Hank actually died in that Carolina town and not in West Virginia, as history has it. Such is the way myth works, especially in the South, where we tend to appropriate the stories we like, giving them our own settings and particulars.

Few American lives lend themselves better to myth than that of Hank Williams. He went, literally, from rags to riches, from a tough Depression-era

Alabama to a Nashville so affluent that he could order tailored California suits and leave huge tips for shoe-shine boys. His passions for whiskey and women pulled against a natural inclination to religion—as if Hank sensed that Americans like some wholesomeness in their heroes, but with a good portion of mischief stirred in. He bucked the system, resisting the domesticity of marriage while offending The Grand Ole Opry until its officials fired him. With his fame snatched away, Hank Williams died mysteriously, on the road, either on the last day of 1952 or the first day of 1953.

It seems that we should be able to chronicle the times and influences of such an important figure, especially because Hank Williams lived so recently and was known by so many. But Hank's rise from obscurity was so fast and his fame so brief that dependable history could hardly keep up. Hank Williams had come and gone before we knew just how much attention he deserved. And with so few facts about a life so dramatic, myth washed in over history. Meanwhile, country music has taken so many turns that, despite Hank's obvious presence in Nashville, identifying all of his legacies is not easy. We really do not know if, given another thirty years, he would have continued to twang away at hard country, glossed himself up for television and the current Nashville scene, or found his way into the outlaw movement of Willie Nelson and Waylon Jennings.

The following pages tell Hank's story, so striking on its own and so bound up in the history of country music. In chapter 1, I provide biographical information. I began the work on it by researching the basic facts available in the numerous official documents that trail through Hank's life, including such things as birth and death certificates, marriage licenses, divorce decrees, and even the prison record of Toby Marshall, the fake doctor who almost certainly wrote the prescription for Hank's last narcotics. With that foundation laid and those facts in hand, I worked through the many volumes and articles that have preceded this book. I also conducted numerous personal interviews and/or corresponded with members of Hank's family, including Taft and Erleen Skipper (Hank's cousins), Irene Williams (Hank's

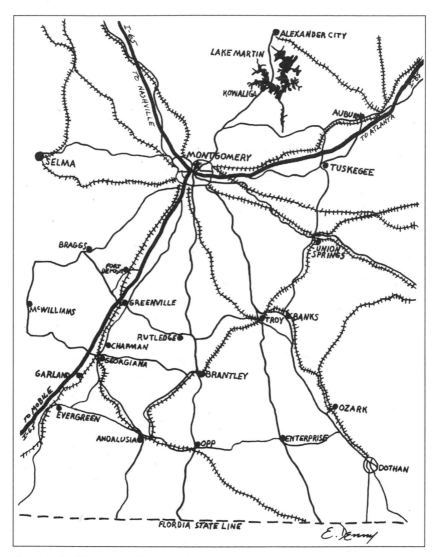

Figure 1. Hank's territory. Illustration by E. Denny.

sister), Leila Williams (Hank's half-sister), and Jett Williams (the daughter born to Hank and Bobbie Jett just a few days after Hank's death), and with such band members and friends as Braxton Schuffert, Jerry Rivers, and Don Helms. I also worked with several highly respected country music scholars, including Bob Pinson of The Country Music Foundation Library and Media Center. My steady effort was to be factual and to include documentation that ties details to sources. This first chapter includes many comments on the music, but its focus is on Hank's life itself. I want readers to see clearly a story marked by drama in almost every detail.

I take up the music in chapter 2, which I believe is the first extended essay of its kind. This chapter lays out Hank's accomplishments and reflects my own appreciation of those achievements. I confirm the familiar argument that Hank Williams, a man who knew almost nothing of the technicalities of music, was largely an inspired and natural genius both as writer and performer. Thus, Hank Williams became the ideal for country music.

In chapter 3, I present the resources. Mainly a discussion and evaluation of bibliography and discography, this chapter ranges over the music, both printed and recorded. In particular, I review the 1998 issue of the ten-compact-disc set "The Complete Hank Williams," produced by Colin Escott, Kira Florita, and The Country Music Foundation. I summarize interviews, survey archival holdings, and review many important essays and books on Hank Williams, including the fairly recent autobiographies of Lycrecia Williams and Jett Williams. I pay much attention to Colin Escott's important 1994 biography, and I note Hank's presence in music, film, and fiction. In the process, this chapter reveals many of the paths I have taken in my work and perhaps can be a guide to future researchers. More than that, though, it demonstrates the huge impact of the singer and songwriter and the remarkable and varied attention that has come to Hank Williams and his music.

Thus, the three chapters of this book are nearly discrete. I did not want to diminish any aspect of my remarkable topic by trying to crowd too much detail into a single chronological sequence. My hope, however, is that the parts come together to shape directly and clearly a full study of Hank Williams, a figure to be respected not just for his defining of country music, but for his contributions to American culture in general.

Hank Williams, *So Lonesome*

I

The Singer: A Biography

If the good Lord's willing, and the creek don't rise...

THE ORIGINS

Nobody bothered to chronicle the childhood of a scruffy, dirt-poor kid growing up in rural Alabama. History became interested in him only after that child came to be famous; and even then it did not rush forward, for few guessed that Hank Williams would be dead before his thirtieth birthday. Time seemed abundant. Hank himself would not have told much anyway. His interviews are few, and they are consistently terse and perfunctory. No Barbara Walters was on hand to draw him out. Childhood was not an especially fond memory for Hank anyway, and he seemed content to let it lie. The result is that his early years are hard to pin down. The information is sketchy and therefore has been particularly susceptible to the stories of friends and relatives, many of them eager to take credit for a career or to protect the image of a hero who was sadly flawed.

If everyone who claims to have given Hank Williams his first guitar had really done so, he might have opened a music store. And if he really became so excited when he got his guitar that he ran out through the yard, jumped on a calf, and twisted its tail, getting thrown and breaking his arm—an injury that kept him from picking any music for a while—I would be surprised. I also find it hard to believe the popular tale that Hank squandered

30¢ on fireworks only to get home to a spanking that set off his purchase in his back pocket. And if all who claimed to be at Mount Olive Baptist Church while a three-year-old Hank Williams sat by his mother as she played the organ, learning there his first rhythm and religion, that sanctuary must have been the size of St. Peter's.

Some facts are clear, however. The parents of Hank Williams were married on 12 November 1916, by Reverend J. C. Dunlap in Butler County, Alabama.[1] Elonzo H. Williams was almost twenty-five, and his bride, Jessie Lillie Belle Skipper, was eighteen. Lon, the youngest of eleven children, was from Lowndes County, the county adjacent to and just south of Montgomery. According to Colin Escott, a recent biographer, Lon's mother, Anne Autrey Williams, committed suicide when the boy was only six years old. His father, Irvin, died eleven years later, making Lon Williams an orphan.[2] But Lon had been basically on his own after quitting school in the sixth grade to begin work as a water boy in the logging camps. He worked his way up in the logging business, eventually becoming a locomotive driver for the W. T. Smith Lumber Company, an outfit that employed as many as 1,200 hands to saw timber and build fruit and produce crates.

His bride, Lillie, was from Butler County, just down the road (one would travel I-65 today) from Lon's haunts. She grew up near Georgiana, a small town about sixty miles south of Montgomery. Lillie was living with her family on a farm and in a house owned by the Mixon family when Lon came to propose. Chet Flippo, another biographer, says that Lon hitched a ride to his intended's house, proposed, and then hitched a ride to the church for the wedding, all in one day.[3] The wedding license was taken out the day before, however, which indicates a little more planning than this story allows.

The scene here is bleak. Times had never been easy in this part of the world, not since the Civil War. The depression that loomed ahead would not have much impact on most of the local folk. Lowndes County—part of a region known as the "Black Belt," not for its considerable black population but for its dark soil—was basically agricultural. Its population of 23,000 in 1930 is about half that today. Butler County was home to 30,000 people in

1930. The following is a promotional description of Butler's largest towns, Greenville and Georgiana, both of which figure in the early years of Hank Williams:

> Greenville, with a population of about 5,000, remains the largest and most important town. It has paved streets, electricity, white way posts and sanitary sewerage, with a number of modern business buildings and homes adjoining the venerable ones of historic construction. Cotton gins, grist mills, a lumber mill, a pants factory, a machine shop, a fertilizer mixing plant and ice factory contribute to an industrial inventory whose overwhelmingly largest item is a 10,000 spindle cotton mill for which the citizens of Greenville made a notable subscription. This is one of the two cities in the United States to have a plant for the preservation of magnolia, beach and oak leaves for decorative purposes. Georgiana, the second ranking community, is a shipping and timber manufacturing center with paved streets, electric lights, a large casket factory, and a municipally owned water system.[4]

It could not have been easy to be so enthusiastic about a small Southern town trying to move from agriculture to industry. We should also keep in mind that, in its beginnings, the Williams family did not exactly live in the city.

The newlyweds spent their first six months with Lillie's family, on the Mixon farm outside Georgiana. The first place they had to themselves was a leased home near Mount Olive Community in Butler County. The double-pen house was in two three-room sections joined by a wide hall, sometimes called a "dog run." The couple, already searching for a steady means of support, opened a store in one side of the house. At the same time, they bought a small patch and started a strawberry business.

Lon's life was tough. The time and place had little to offer, especially to an uneducated man; and his wife, who was capable of surviving on her own, offered no sympathy. His life was complicated when he was drafted into the military, where he served from 9 July 1918 through 26 June 1919, part of that time in France. Just what happened to him overseas is not entirely clear. Jay Caress reports that he was shell-shocked and gassed, whereas Chet Flippo, apparently working from an obscure interview with Lon, says that he was injured in a fight with another soldier over a French girl.[5] Colin Escott prefers the Flippo version.[6] But Leila Williams Griffin, Lon's daughter by a later marriage and thus Hank's half-sister, told me in a letter of 18 April 1982 that her father fell from a truck, breaking his collarbone and suffering a blow to the head that would give him problems for years to come. Lon Williams, whatever the cause, came home from Europe a nervous and unsteady man who was no match for either a large, aggressive wife or a mean economy.

Lon's difficulties increased as his children were born. The first infant died. Then Irene was born on 8 August 1922, and just over a year later, on 17 September 1923, Lillie gave birth to Hank Williams. One rumor is that Lon wanted to name the boy King, but that Lillie held out for Hiram. The handwritten birth certificate, which was not filed until 1 March 1934, misspells the child's name as "Hiriam."[7] So Hank was to be Hiram, probably until 1937 when the family moved to Montgomery. By then, Hank Snow was an influence, and Hank Williams might have liked the cowboy image better than that of outback Alabama.

The picture is this: an already poor Alabama getting set for a depression, a husband and father weak because of his war injury, a dominant wife and mother, and two children. The best facsimile of their life as a young family is probably in the photographs that Walker Evans took for James Agee's text in the classic *Let Us Now Praise Famous Men*.[8] The pictures of Alabama in the early 1930s include an excellent one of a double-pen house that could have been Hank's, and the families depicted could have been his as well. "Poor but proud" would do as a general description, but poverty had the upper hand.

Life of this sort leads one to pursue every possible means of making a little money. A small farm may help feed a family, but hard cash—and what it would buy—looks all the better for its absence. Lon worked off and

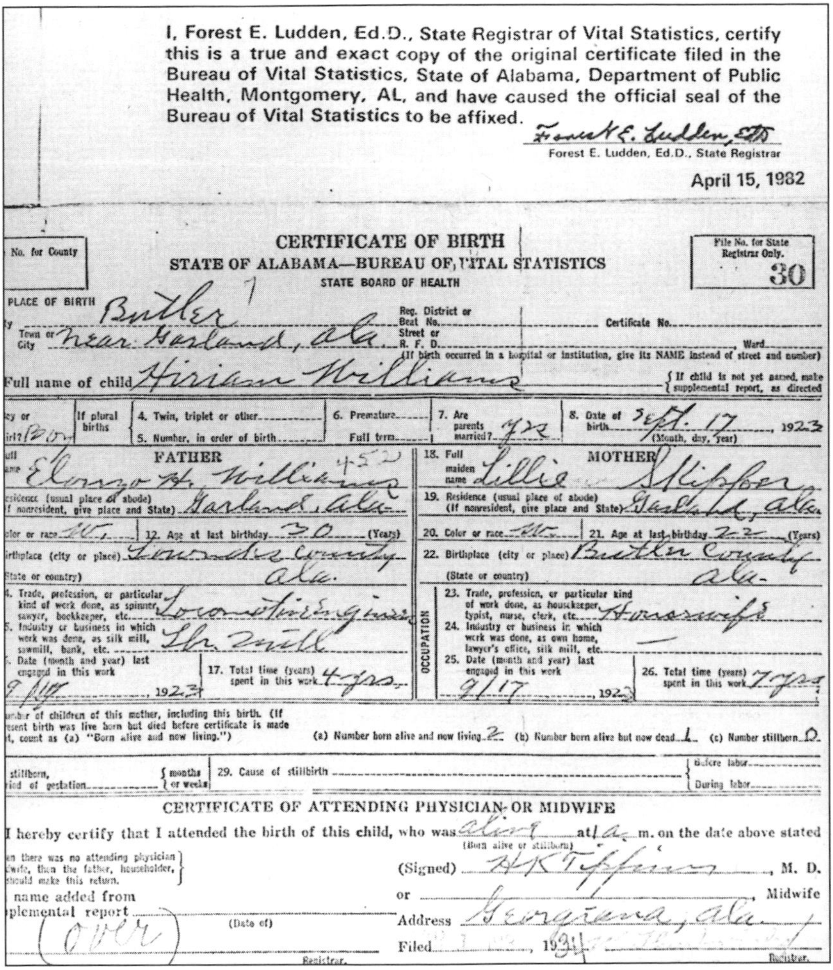

I, Forest E. Ludden, Ed.D., State Registrar of Vital Statistics, certify this is a true and exact copy of the original certificate filed in the Bureau of Vital Statistics, State of Alabama, Department of Public Health, Montgomery, AL, and have caused the official seal of the Bureau of Vital Statistics to be affixed.

Forest E. Ludden, Ed.D., State Registrar

April 15, 1982

CERTIFICATE OF BIRTH
STATE OF ALABAMA—BUREAU OF VITAL STATISTICS
STATE BOARD OF HEALTH

No. for County — File No. for State Registrar Only. 30

PLACE OF BIRTH — County: Butler — Town or City: near Garland, Ala.

Full name of child: Hiriam Williams

Sex of child: Boy — Are parents married?: Yes — Date of birth: Sept. 17, 1923

FATHER — Full name: Elonzo H. Williams — Residence: Garland, Ala. — Color or race: W. — Age at last birthday: 30 (Years) — Birthplace: Lowndes County, Ala. — Trade, profession, or particular kind of work done: Locomotive Engineer — Industry or business in which work was done: Lbr. mill — Date (month and year) last engaged in this work: 9 ..., 1923 — Total time (years) spent in this work: 4 yrs.

MOTHER — Full maiden name: Lillie Skipper — Residence: Garland, Ala. — Color or race: W. — Age at last birthday: 22 (Years) — Birthplace: Butler County, Ala. — Trade, profession, or particular kind of work done: Housewife — Date last engaged in this work: 9/17, 1923 — Total time (years) spent in this work: 7 yrs.

Number of children of this mother, including this birth: (a) Number born alive and now living 2 (b) Number born alive but now dead 1 (c) Number stillborn 0

CERTIFICATE OF ATTENDING PHYSICIAN OR MIDWIFE

I hereby certify that I attended the birth of this child, who was alive at 1 a.m. on the date above stated

(Signed) H K Tippins, M. D.

Address: Georgiana, Ala.

Filed ..., 1934

(OVER)

Figure 2. Hank's birth certificate, which lists the child's name as "Hiriam Williams."

on at the lumber yards. He and Lillie opened another store. They tried the strawberry business on land burned out with cotton. Lillie worked as a nurse, took in sewing, worked at the cannery, and gardened. Hank and Irene sold peanuts and seeds and picked cotton and strawberries. Hank delivered groceries and shined shoes. Pursuit of a better life meant many moves—to places like Chapman, Garland, McWilliams, and Georgiana—all before 1935, when the family moved to Greenville. Two years later, the Williams moved to Montgomery.

Lon had trouble keeping up. In 1929, probably in November, he left home. He was not in Garland when Hank's cousin, Taft Skipper, and his bride, Erleen, moved in with Lillie, Irene, Hank, and Grandma Skipper in December 1929. Lon apparently had begun a long series of stays in Veterans Administration hospitals. Leila Williams Griffin, in the letter noted above, explains that the blow Lon suffered in France produced an aneurysm close to his brain, paralyzing his face and destroying his ability to speak. The VA diagnosed dementia praecox, and in the early 1930s, Lon began receiving total disability. Because of this particular diagnosis, the money was sent directly to his family, who probably got a retroactive, lump-sum payment and then a regular monthly installment. The new income was fine, but it was a steady reminder that Hank, like Lon himself, would grow up practically fatherless.

Lillie managed fairly well without her husband. When their place in Georgiana burned down, she was quick to find another house, this one on Rose Street and large enough for her to inaugurate her career as manager of boardinghouses. Her resourcefulness and her instinct for financial matters were not always attractive, but they kept things going. She might have found a comfortable place in a rising mercantile class had she not paused to manage a famous son. Interviews with neighbors and family produce different opinions of Lillie. Some found her honest and hardworking, if given to the dollar. Others who came to know her after Hank had established his career found her pushy and greedy. The point seems to be that early in her marriage her survival instincts were attractive. Later, as her son became better known, those same energies became less appealing as they went toward making certain that she realized every dollar possible from his life and death.

As both child and adult, Hank Williams was frail and withdrawn. Roger Williams's interviews with various relatives tell us as much:

> From the start, Hank was a thin and sickly boy. His sister, Irene, describes him as "pretty frail. He was no athlete. Every time he tried sports, it seemed, he broke something." One such effort, perhaps at ice skating, resulted in a ruptured disk, contributing to back problems that were to plague him most of his adult life. A cousin who spent a great deal of time with young Hank, J. C. McNeil, remembers him as "a real loner. He never was a happy boy, in a way. He didn't laugh and carry on like other children. It seemed like somethin' was always on his mind."[9]

A difficult life and a domineering mother explain some of this, but an additional factor was involved: Hank Williams had chronic back problems. The narcotics that he came to depend on, which probably were at least partially responsible for his death, were allowed at first because of his ailment. One story attributes the problem to an ice-skating accident, but the skates would have been as scarce as ice in Hank's world. Another, reported both by Roger Williams and Jay Caress, is that Hank ran away West at the age of seventeen, got drunk, entered a rodeo, and was thrown from a horse.[10] Documenting this episode seems to be impossible, although the story reflects Hank's fascination with cowboys and booze. By far the best explanation of his problem lies in the symptoms of spina bifida occulta in Hank's medical reports and in his autopsy.[11] Spina bifida occulta is a birth defect; the vertebral arches fail to unite and thus allow the spinal cord to herniate, to extend outward from the spine. The most serious version of this problem, known as spina bifida, creates a large protrusion or tumor on the back and can cause partial or complete paralysis as well as the loss of sensation and sphincter control. Hank's type was not so severe. There evidently was no external growth, but even the lesser version (the occulta) can leave a mark on the back and effect the lower extremities. The ailment is progressive and thus explains some of Hank's problems, especially his occasional paralysis, along with his trouble with sports as a child. Alcohol and drugs were the villains in the end, but only the spina bifida occulta seems to explain Hank's enduring pain.

This kind of spinal herniation makes nerves particularly vulnerable to injury. The most ordinary fall could cause real trouble, not to mention a fall from ice skates or a rodeo horse. That a variety of falls, which only aggravated his problem, got credit for the problem itself is not surprising. We might like to think that an early diagnosis and appropriate surgery could have repaired Hank's back and perhaps changed his life entirely. But such an opportunity was rare during his childhood; an open spinal column in the days before the regular use of antibiotics would have been disastrous. For Hank Williams, fate designed a time and place that admitted little relief from a serious and painful ailment. At the same time, though, that fate may have led Hank Williams to his music because his bad health kept him from some of the activities typical of boys growing up.

Not everything in Hank's early years was gloomy. Lillie provided for him well enough, and he seems to have had a particularly good year in 1934–1935, when he lived with his cousins, J. C. and Walt McNeil, near Fountain in Monroe County. He had swapped homes with their sister, Opal, who had moved into Georgiana to live with Lillie and finish high school. The McNeils lived in the Pool lumber camp, in a boxcar that had been converted into living quarters. This home was nothing unfamiliar or embarrassing because many of the company's employees lived in the cars, which could be moved easily as the camp followed timber. The benefits for Hank were several. He and the McNeil boys were good pals, which meant much to the loner, Hank Williams. The McNeils had more of a family life than Hank was used to, and by all reports they were kind to their guest. Certainly Hank did not have to hit the streets to hawk whatever goods Lillie had come up with for him to sell. But perhaps the most attractive aspect was that Hank was not socially inferior among the McNeils and their friends. Their neighbors were all alike; they worked for the same company, and the

Figure 3. Hank at thirteen. Photograph courtesy of Bruce Gidoll.

neighborhood moved as one. Here Hank was not the fatherless kid from the next town, shining shoes in the barbershop.

Hank took to the basic item on the McNeil social calendar, the Saturday night dances that the lumber camps loved. He liked the live country music and the frolicking that went with it. He was not ignorant of music at this point; his mother had been the church organist, and she had Hank on the organ bench beside her for services. But the Pool camp may have been the place where he first heard music played in the context of so much fun. The people in the logging camps knew how to have a good time, and part of their method, of course, involved strong drink.

The irony of drinking in many rural areas, especially in the South, is that most know that it goes on, but few see it happen. Drink is not so much a social matter as a preparation for social matters. It happens, and those who are courteous pretend that it does not happen. All of this means hiding the booze, drinking it in the woods or in a car, and then stashing it away to return to the party. Kids, then, have easy access to it, much easier than if the drinking were public. All that a child has to do is observe and then partake of the elixir. The eleven-year-old Hank apparently caught on to the code quickly. It is not easy to identify a particular point where his alcoholism started; the problems were probably built into him, for Hank Williams seems to have been highly susceptible to drink. Had he not gotten into it at the McNeil's, he would have gotten into it elsewhere. But he did come home from their place with some new knowledge. He must have been aware of the deficiencies in his own family life, perhaps even aware that Lillie was a little exploitative. Hank knew how much fun the music could be, and he may have associated the whiskey with the good times.

THE FAME

One of the best things hard times can produce is music. They generated gospel and the blues for poor blacks, and they produced country for poor whites. In fact, singers establishing themselves in these genres today, when the socioeconomic implications have faded, had still better be able to convince audiences that authentic suffering stands behind their work. Hank Williams had no trouble providing that history. He took up his trade with full and legitimate credentials. Alabama in the 1930s could produce as much music as the dust bowl, a West Virginia coal mine, a cotton field, or a New Orleans slum.

Hank was a natural, and much of his ability seemed to be innate. Maybe he inherited it from his grandfather Skipper, a blacksmith who supposedly composed some rhythmic songs for his hammering. Perhaps he got some of it from his mother, who pumped away at those four-square hymns at the Baptist Church. Certainly, he had found plenty of music among his relatives, the McNeil's, both at the lumber camp parties and at home, where Mrs. McNeil played the guitar. Hank seemed to come out of that particular year ready to make his own songs.

When Roger Williams tried to find out just who presented Hank with his first instrument, he got enough answers to confuse the issue for good. Lillie claimed credit, saying she bought Hank a $3.50 guitar, paid off at 50¢ a month, to encourage him to do better work in school. The good son Hank confirmed his mother's part later, although he mentioned nothing about school. Fred Thigpen, who ran the Ford place in Georgiana, says that he bought Hank his first guitar, a $2.50 number, from Warren's store. Others report that Jim Warren himself gave Hank the guitar.[12] The only consistency is the chronology: Hank started picking when he was about twelve years old. Should the argument about who was responsible continue, we might note that Hank was not destined to become any great picker anyway. Basic rhythm was about all he ever managed, and even at that he was sometimes encouraged to leave his guitar at home when he came to recording sessions. Among his numerous recordings, he had only one brief guitar solo, that on "My Bucket's Got a Hole in It."

Hank did get a little instruction from an old-time fiddler, Cade Durham, who ran Georgiana's shoe shop and had a string band fairly well known in those parts. No doubt, he also picked up some help from the street singers who were so common in that time and place. After all, Hank certainly moved among them on his various missions for Lillie. He probably came across a singer named Dove Hazelip and another, Connie "Big Day" McKee. But the biggest influence in this part of Hank's life was the black street singer Rufe Payne, known generally as "Tee Tot." He was from Greenville, just up the L&N Railroad line, but he drifted down to hustle Georgiana occasionally.

As I have mentioned already, country singers work hard to establish authenticity. One way to do this is to claim tutelage from black street

Figure 4. Thigpen's Log Cabin, near Georgiana, Alabama. This is one of the honky-tonks that Hank played regularly. Photograph by E. Denny.

singers, perhaps the most authentic of musicians. But I think it important to note that Rufe Payne was real. Colin Escott has identified him, even to the point of finding notice of his death in Montgomery Charity Hospital on 17 March 1939. Escott goes on to suggest, logically I think, that "Tee Tot" was an ironic diminutive of "Teetotaler."[13] So again, Hank's country influences seem to be genuine.

Rufe was a beggar with talent, the kind who continued well through my own childhood in the 1940s and 1950s, although social programs and ordinances against begging finally took care of them in the 1960s and 1970s. Many of them were handicapped—blind men, amputees, or winos—who tried to stop passersby long enough to perform and to collect a few coins, often in a tin cup tied to the neck of a guitar. The problem, of course, came in stopping people long enough for the show. That called for more than simple songs; it called for the showmanship that Rufe had mastered—some jokes, some shuffling, some music, and no small amount of flattery of the crowd that might well mean sustenance. Hank learned some music from Rufe, but maybe even better, he learned showmanship. The interesting point here, I believe, is that as Rufe marked some of Hank's authenticity, so would Hank himself, many years later, become the reference point for up and coming country singers. Again and again, in efforts to prove their sincerity, country singers cite Hank Williams as an inspiration.

The fate that had played some mean tricks on Hank suddenly served him well in 1935 when he, Lillie, and Irene moved up to Greenville, Rufe's hometown. Hank had almost constant access to his mentor now; he was much on the streets. Lillie was a demanding mother, and his stay with the McNeil's probably had led him to realize that life with her was not exactly cozy. Hank was twelve, into his adolescence, hard to keep up with, streetwise, and tall enough to pass for an adult. He was to spend more time with Rufe Payne.

They had much in common: music, of course, and a sense of the urgency of survival. Neither one of them really belonged to a normal social order, and neither took much to ordinary, day-to-day work. If Lillie was giving Hank a bad time, he could stay with Rufe and enjoy the commiseration. Unfortunately, Rufe solaced himself with whiskey as well as with music. Thus, Hank had his second major encounter with alcohol. Rufe taught him plenty of music, and in the bargain Rufe gave him access to booze, a place to drink it, and a place to sleep it off out of the way of Lillie Williams.

Hank was now ready to travel, and once again, one of his family's many moves was to serve his purposes. On 10 July 1937, Lillie, Irene, and the fourteen-year-old Hank Williams headed for Montgomery, a hot, flat town of 75,000 people who knew plenty about country music and the home of a really good country radio station, WSFA. Lillie went straight into the boardinghouse business at 114 South Perry Street. Irene made lunches to peddle around town, and Hank was supposed to be back shining shoes and selling peanuts. Actually, he spent most of his time looking for a way to pick up where he had left off with Rufe Payne. He was ready to get off the streets and onto the stage, ready to be discovered. Hank met a young cowboy singer, Braxton Schuffert, who had his own radio show and who performed with Smith "Hezzy" Adair. Schuffert, who was to become one of Hank's most dependable friends, made Hank Williams even more anxious to be a professional performer.

He found his chance late in the fall of 1937. The Empire Theatre ran a sort of Bijou operation: full entertainment for the kids—movies of the Bomba and Tex Ritter type, serials, cartoons—and a talent show, usually dominated by spoon players, pantomimists, and yo-yo artists. Hank entered the talent show, singing his own composition, "The WPA Blues," which was obviously based on Riley Puckett's "Dissatisfied" (1930) and which went like this:

> I got a home in Montgomery
> A place I like to stay
> But I have to work for the WPA
> And I'm dissatisfied—I'm dissatisfied.

That tune never made it onto any of his records, nor does it turn up in the Hank Williams catalog. But the performance is a good place to start Hank's career because it identified what Hank was to come to do so well—sing about a tough life that he shared with his audiences. He won first prize in the talent show and left the Empire Theatre that night with $15. He must have been trying to calculate how many pairs of shoes he would have had to shine to get that kind of money. And more good news was at hand: Lillie, with her sharp eye for either talent or money, inaugurated her career as promoter of her son by giving him a new Gibson guitar as an advance on his Christmas present.

None of this was doing Hank much good at Baldwin Junior High School, on South McDonough Street, where he was struggling with the seventh grade. But it helped get him on WSFA, where he became The Singing Kid with Dad Crysel's band. He was a big success and soon had his own fifteen-minute program that came on twice a week.

This arrangement established a pattern that was to become a part of Hank Williams's life. WSFA had a fairly large broadcast area: its 3,000 watts carried programs throughout southern Alabama and into neighboring states. The result was a good constituency for live appearances around the countryside. The Louisiana Hayride and The Grand Ole Opry, which lay ahead for Hank, worked the same way. A performer was promoted over the air and then hit the road, showing up at every schoolhouse and barn dance he could book, letting fans see in the flesh the singer and composer of songs they had heard on the air waves. He headed back to the radio station for more promotion and then back on the road. Television would eventually cut down on the burden of travel, but Hank Williams would not live long enough to enjoy that benefit.

Going on the road meant that Hank needed a band; not even Hank Williams could carry an entire road show by himself. Hank had already lured Hezzy Adair away from Braxton Schuffert; Hezzy, an orphan who had been living with the Schufferts, had moved into Lillie's boardinghouse, where the supervision was not so constant. He could crack the jokes expected of a country bass player; and Braxton, who booked the first dates for Hank and the band, filled in occasionally on lead guitar. Irene served as vocalist and ticket-taker, and Freddy Beech joined up as fiddler. Chet Flippo, who includes a good photograph of the band in his book, notes that Beech, married and the father of two children, was, at nineteen, the oldest member of the group.[14] They played, Hezzy told his jokes, the band chattered with Hank, and then followed a moment of sacred music—at least until they started getting into the honky-tonks. The idea was to entertain in any way possible. Rufe Payne would have understood perfectly. And Hank would carry on that pattern with his most famous version of the band, The Drifting Cowboys.

The band personnel was not so crucial at this point because Hank was obviously the drawing card, and it shifted regularly. Don Helms, the first of the permanent Drifting Cowboys, did not join the group until 1943. The

WSFA studio photograph of the Cowboys, in fact, shows an outfit entirely different from the one just described. This group had Mexican Charlie Mays on fiddle, Shorty Seals on bass, Indian Joe Hatcher playing lead guitar, and Boots Harris on steel guitar, an instrument that came to identify Hank's sound best.

Hank had good control of his band. They were not much of a draw without him, and besides, Lillie's boardinghouse, recently moved to 236 Catoma Street, was a good place to hole up. They must have had a good time: men their age, most of them used to precious little money, on the road with a man who was to become the best ever in country music. One catch, though: if Hank had control of the band, Lillie had control of Hank. Maybe she sensed his lack of direction, maybe she was interested in his well-being, maybe she could see the money to be made. Whatever the reasons, Lillie went at Hank's business with dedication—providing room and board to the crew, arranging engagements, collecting admission (usually 25¢), and trying to keep Hank (already deep into drink long before he was old enough to buy whiskey) sober enough to perform.

According to Flippo, Lillie made another important contribution: she had a pretty good right cross.[15] And every punch helped in the spots Hank and the Drifting Cowboys came to play. They did the schoolhouses and other respectable places, but they also played the roadhouses, the gutbuckets—in places like Rutledge, Evergreen, Andalusia, Fort Deposit, and, of course, Montgomery itself—where the major pastimes were drinking, dancing, picking up women, and then fighting over the women just picked up. The standard saying in all of these places is that the owners have to sweep out the eyeballs every morning.

The band was not exempt from the fighting, and places like these have actually strung chicken wire between the customers and the performers. Hank supposedly equipped his band with blackjacks on one occasion. He himself often carried a pistol, a habit that got more and more dangerous as his drinking increased. Also, Hank evidently broke more than one guitar on a jealous boyfriend. The leg off a steel guitar was not a bad weapon; neither was the steel bar used to chord the instrument. According to an interview with Sammy Pruett, a longtime Drifting Cowboy from Alabama, Hank was using the bar on a customer "when another local guy coming to Hank's assistance almost cut the first guy in two. He had to hold his guts in. They took Hank into court the next day, but the judge let him off. Hell, it wasn't his fault." In another tale, a customer bit out a chunk of Hank's eyebrow.[16] Stories like this wind through Hank's history. Not all of them are true, but they capture the texture of many years of Hank Williams's life as a performer.

Life took a strange and quick turn in the fall of 1942 when Hank left Montgomery. One might suppose that the honky-tonk circuit had gotten to him, that the drinking and fighting had accumulated and taken their toll. But the likelihood is that Hank was restless. His father, Lon, had been home briefly after his 1939 release from the hospital, only to leave again in a divorce. Lillie had remarried, this time to a Mr. J. C. Bozard. But not even new romance could keep her from being a problem for Hank. He was a successful performer, a man able to make his own way, and yet one who had to report to his mother, let her count his change and hand out his assignments.

Many of Hank's acquaintances had gone into the service by now. Irene had left to work at Gunter Field. School was not going well; his vision was bad, and staying awake in classes after playing half the night was hard. He was nineteen and only in the ninth grade when he decided to give up education for good. Lillie did not try to stop him; later, in her book on Hank, she justified the parental indulgence by saying that "too much book learning might have spoiled the wonderful, natural flow of his song-words."[17] The army rejected him because of his back problems. Hank—maybe a little embarrassed by this and maybe just feeling some need to act in the midst of the turmoil of the times—headed for Mobile, the next real city down the way.

In Mobile, Hank lived with his uncle, Bob Skipper, and he worked for the Alabama Drydock and Shipbuilding Company as a shipfitter's helper (at 66¢ per hour, according to company records) and later as a welding trainee. He would be there until August 1944. Just what went on in Mobile is not recorded. We might want to see the stint as meditative, a period when Hank Williams got himself ready to charge the music scene once more. Such may have been the indirect effect, but Hank's life was never so highly designed. Besides, the break was not quite so clean. Hank's record in the shipyards was short of exemplary, probably because, even while in Mobile, he kept up with his band and played dates out of Montgomery. Don Helms, in fact, is certain that he first joined the Drifting Cowboys in 1943, right in the middle of Hank's term with the Alabama Drydock and Shipbuilding Company. Hank kept the road from Mobile to Montgomery well traveled.

The deal seemed to be a pretty good one for Hank, as if it took all those miles to separate him from Lillie's dominance. And we might wonder why he came home. Lillie claimed she went to get him. She said she booked shows for Hank for sixty days straight and then drove to Mobile and brought Hank back. She quoted Hank, upon seeing his mother and the schedule of shows: "Thank God, mother. You have made me the happiest boy in the world."[18] Hank was no boy now, however, and imagining any such conversation between this mother and son is difficult. He could be contrite, but I cannot believe he was so thrilled by the rescue. Besides, Lillie botched her tale by saying that Hank was gone for only three weeks; Hank had been away for nearly two years. But Lillie always loved to think that Hank was affectionate, that he could not get along without her, that she was responsible for his fame.

My impression is that this was a period of real struggle for Hank Williams, although we could say that about the singer's entire life. But this particular version of the struggle had him caught between regular work and the career in music that he wanted, between the independence of Mobile and the uneasy security of life in Montgomery with Lillie. Clearly, he was drinking hard. Audrey Williams, in her fragmented and unpublished memoir, said that Hank had "drifted along like this for three or four years with musicians quitting and new ones coming in." She noted as well that Hank had become so undependable that WSFA had cancelled his show.[19] Lillie, whatever her full motives, seems to have been trying to salvage her son and his career. And she was getting some help, as inept as it turned out to be.

Audrey Mae Sheppard Guy had entered the drama. About half a year older than Hank, she was from a community known as Enon, just outside a little town called Banks. The place is about 50 miles southeast of Montgomery. She was the oldest of three daughters who were, stories have it, closely guarded by their father, Charley Sheldon Sheppard, a hard-drinking and not very prosperous peanut and cotton grower. Charley had good reason to keep an eye on Audrey. Many years later, Hank Jr. describes her: "Audrey Sheppard was beautiful—long blond hair and a figure that could melt the wax off a Dixie Cup at fifty feet. And she had drive, something that Hank was sadly lacking."[20] When she was a senior in high school, just before turning eighteen, she had eloped with Erskine Guy, a neighborhood boyfriend. She reappeared at Charley's, in the summer of 1941, pregnant with Lycrecia Ann Guy who would be born on 13 August 1941. Erskine Guy had evaporated, gone after the proverbial loaf of bread; he would turn up eventually in the military overseas.

Audrey, in the memoir mentioned above, says that she met Hank late in the summer of 1943. She and her Aunt Ethel were on their way to a club in Troy, Alabama, when they passed a dilapidated medicine show in Banks. Hank was performing and then peddling herbs at intermission. He joined the two women for the evening and asked Audrey to come back the next day. She found him drunk and dirty when she drove up at noon. She sobered him up, made him bathe, listened to his account of his troubles, and fell in love—partly with Hank Williams, partly with the prospect of getting off the farm, partly with the misguided notion that she herself might have a career in music.[21] She would be living at Lillie's Montgomery boardinghouse before long and was almost certainly the main reason for Hank's return from Mobile, which must have rankled Lillie.

The psychology here is interesting. In the most obvious matter, the fragile and drifting Hank Williams had formed another attachment to a woman who wanted both to take care of him and to take advantage of him.

Audrey had much in common with Lillie, enough to keep the two women at each other's throats for about a decade. Maybe their contentions over him gave the emotionally isolated son and lover some kind of twisted reassurance. Their main concern was with Hank's drinking, and they fought hard to keep him from it. Maybe this attention helped drive Hank more deeply into his habit. Being the bad boy might have paid off short term; it would destroy him in the end.

More subtle and interesting, I think, is that the relationship with Audrey began a pattern in Hank's life. As a musician rambling in and out of honky-tonks, he knew plenty of women. But he formed only three truly significant attachments: with Audrey, with Bobbie Jett, and with Billie Jean Eshliman. When these women met Hank, each already had a child. I do not speculate here toward some psychological syndrome, but these relationships seem to point to the great loneliness of Hank Williams, a man who at some level wanted a stable life with family, a want that his history and his dependencies would never allow.

When Hank got back from Mobile in the fall of 1944, though, he was ready to get serious about his music and his romance. The two charms merged as Audrey, ambitious would-be singer, came to be vocalist with the Drifting Cowboys. She could hardly carry a tune, and she proved to be no songwriter, but the business of being able to perform with his true love overwhelmed Hank Williams. Besides, she was aggressive enough to take over when Hank was drunk.

Audrey formally divorced Erskine Guy on 5 December 1944, a few months after Hank had moved back to Montgomery from Mobile. The divorce decree, issued in Pike County, Alabama, cited Guy for "voluntary abandonment" and made him responsible for financing the "support of his dependent child...Lycrecia Ann Guy, age nearly four years." He was to pay a monthly sum equal to whatever the War Department allowed military personnel for support of a dependent child.[22] In short, Guy was to continue the check that Audrey was already getting for Lycrecia. According to Lycrecia, Audrey always denied receiving any support from Guy.[23]

The State of Alabama, Pike County

CIRCUIT COURT, IN EQUITY

AUDREY GUY
....Complainant

VS.

ERSKINE(JAMES E.) GUY ....Respondent

This cause coming on to be heard was submitted upon Bill of Complaint, ~~THRXXXYXXXXXXX~~ on answer

and Testimony as noted by the............**complainant's attorney**....................and upon consideration thereof, the Court is of the opinion that the Complainant is entitled to the relief prayed for in said bill.

It is therefore ordered, adjudged and decreed by the Court that the bonds of matrimony heretofore existing between the Complainant and Defendant be, and the same are hereby dissolved, and that the said..................

AUDREY GUY ....is forever divorced from the said

ERSKINE (JAMES E.) GUY ....

for and on account of ....VOLUNTARY ABANDONMENT..........

And, it appearing from the files that the respondent has agreed in writing, said writing duly filed, that the present support for his dependent child(the child of the parties hereto) Lycrecia Ann Guy, age nearly four years, be fixed at the amount allowed by the Government or War Department for a dependent child, xx or allotted for the support of such child, it is, therefore, further, ORDERED, ADJUDGED, AND DECREED, by the Court, that the complainant Audrey Guy, for the use and benefit of said minor child Lycrecia Ann Guy, have and recover of said respondent, JAMES E.(Erskine) Guy a monthly sum in the same amount allowed by the Government, or War Department for the support of a dependent minor child,

It is further ordered, adjudged and decreed that neither party to this suit shall again marry except to each other until sixty days after the rendition of this decree, and that if appeal is taken within sixty days, neither party shall again marry except to each other during the pendency of said appeal.

It is further ordered that....................**Audrey Guy**......................... be, and............**is**....................hereby permitted to again contract marriage upon the payment of the cost of this suit, that Respondent shall................................be permitted to marry again.

It is further ordered that....................**Audrey Guy**.........................
the..........**complainant**..........................pay the cost herein to be taxed, for which execution may issue.

This..........**5th**..........day of..........**December**..........194..**4**..

....
Judge Circuit Court, in Equity.

I, ..., Register of the Circuit

Court for............................County, Alabama, do hereby certify that the foregoing is a correct copy of the original decree rendered by the Judge of the Circuit Court in the above stated cause, which said decree is on file and enrolled in my office, and the cost has been paid.

Witness my hand and seal this the........................day of......................................., 194........

....
Register of Circuit Court, in Equity.

Figure 5. Audrey's divorce decree from Erskine Guy. It notes the couple's child, Lycrecia, and the terms of her support. Granted on 5 December 1944, the decree stipulates that neither party could marry again, except to each other, for sixty days.

Audrey's divorce decree includes the statement standard in Alabama: "It is further ordered, adjudged and decreed that neither party to this suit shall again marry except to each other until sixty days after the rendition of this decree." Ten days later, on 15 December 1944, Audrey and Hank applied for a marriage license in Andalusia, Alabama. Hank filled out the form, listing himself as a "Band Leader," white, and age twenty-one. He passed the venereal disease test, which was not required of Audrey, given by Dr. L. L. Parker. Audrey indicates clearly on the form that she had been divorced on 5 December 1944. The notary, Annie R. Broxson, evidently unaware of Alabama's sixty-day reconciliation period, approved the license. The pair married that same day, in a Texaco station outside Andalusia. The Drifting Cowboys, who supposedly had to chip in to pay Justice of the Peace M. A. Boyett, were witnesses.[24] Hank and Audrey went home to Lillie's boardinghouse. They did not file their license and certificate for nearly two months. They did not need to rush, however, because due to the violation of Audrey's period of reconciliation, their marriage was to be one of common law anyway.

Life must have looked pretty good to Hank now. He had Audrey, apparently for keeps, and his band was getting solid. Don Helms and Sammy Pruett, who were to be part of the most famous version of the Drifting Cowboys, were both on hand. The money was better now: Hank could pay a man $10 for a performance, and they were out three or four nights a week. Lillie had a decent place for them to stay, although it did not come free of charge. Audrey was taking on some of her mother-in-law's chores with the band—handling bookings, keeping up with the money, taking tickets, performing, and especially keeping the show rolling when Hank did not quite make it.

Country music was spreading in popularity, and Hank was having more and more success. But his domestic life was getting messier by the day. He had two women to take care of him now—or two women to fight over the benefits of his success. And by all accounts, Lillie and Audrey fought with real punches. Hank seemed to be getting famous for his two caretakers,

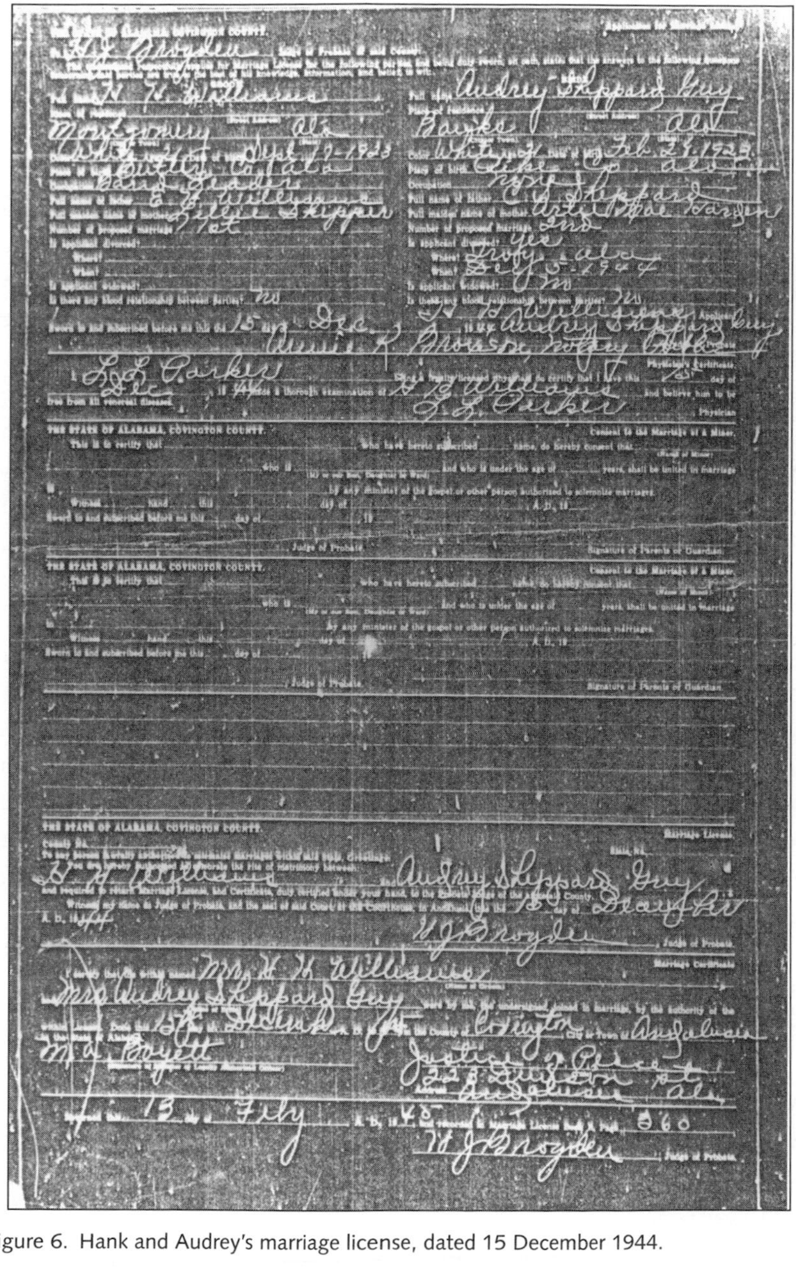

THE STATE OF ALABAMA, COVINGTON COUNTY.

Full name: Audrey Sheppard Guy

THE STATE OF ALABAMA, COVINGTON COUNTY. Consent to the Marriage of a Minor.

THE STATE OF ALABAMA, COVINGTON COUNTY. Consent to the Marriage of a Minor.

THE STATE OF ALABAMA, COVINGTON COUNTY. Marriage License.

Audrey Sheppard Guy

Judge of Probate.

Marriage Certificate.

Mrs Audrey Sheppard Guy

Judge of Probate.

Figure 6. Hank and Audrey's marriage license, dated 15 December 1944.

and that took the edge off his progress. Chet Flippo catches it well: "The better Hank became, the less he seemed to care about his career. Lillie and Audrey both tried lecturing him and they both received hostile stares for their trouble. They resolved that it was their duty to stroke the career along, since Hank wasn't responsible enough to do so. Audrey, too, still had designs of making it big as a singer herself."[25] The scene was tense: Audrey and Lillie were not getting along but banded together to push Hank. Hank apparently resented them for their trouble. He was drinking far too much; his back was hurting; the drink and the back together may have caused him some impotence; Audrey nagged. Bernice Hilburn Turner, a native of Arkansas who played rhythm guitar for Hank in 1945 and 1946 says the scene was rough. She and her husband Doyle, a steel guitarist who took over that instrument when Don Helms was drafted, lived with the band at Lillie's boardinghouse. In a 15 September 2000 interview, she recalls ambiguously that "Hank was not a naturally ornery drunk, even though he got into a lot of bar fights." Audrey's complaints were more about drinking than about other women, Turner adds before going on to say that the Williams's fights were mild compared to those she had with Doyle, another alcoholic. Turner remembers shooting at Doyle and hitting him with a chisel.[26]

All of this went on in the boardinghouse, with a handful of strangers and some of the Drifting Cowboys to witness. Lycrecia, who lived with her grandparents, Shelton and Artie Mae Sheppard, during the first two years of Hank and Audrey's marriage, visited enough to get a taste of the turmoil. She would see a lot more of it when she moved in full-time in 1946. Meanwhile, Lillie's domestic life was not exactly even. Mr. Bozard had fled her physical attacks, and she took on her next husband, W. W. Stone, one of the more attractive boarders.

Being on the road must have brought some relief to Hank and the band, but that had its problems too—the alcohol, the domestic squabbling, and especially Audrey's desire to sing. She simply had no talent, a fact well rep-

Figure 7. Hank and Lillie Williams. Photograph courtesy of Bruce Gidoll.

resented in the Metro recording "Mr. and Mrs. Hank Williams" (M-572), in which she destroys every melody. I got these responses when I asked Jerry Rivers and Don Helms about the matter:

JERRY: Well, yes. It wasn't comfortable having a woman along, especially the boss's wife. We had to watch what we said. And not only that, she wasn't a good singer. You could kick off a song, and she might not sing in the same key. Who was I to say, "Hey, you got it in the wrong key?" It was uncomfortable.

D O N : She just wasn't professional. She cramped our style. She cramped Hank's
style. He told me one time, "It's bad to have a wife who wants to sing, but
it's hell to have one who wants to sing and can't."[27]

In the midst of all this, Hank was still trying to carry on his career. He
had his daily, one o'clock radio show on WSFA again and usually followed
it by a stand in a joint somewhere in the outback full of drunks perfectly
willing to bite off an ear or slice you in half with a jackknife. No one who
knew Hank Williams was surprised to find him entering the hospital in
Prattville, Alabama for his first treatment for alcoholism. He was twenty-
two years old.

In spite of his many problems, though, Hank had been writing a good
bit of music. "The WPA Blues" must have been ringing in his ears. He had
some time for writing in Mobile and some time while lying around Lillie's
boardinghouse, listening to the women scrap with each other or complain
about his drinking. His songs were not bad. And by the time World War II
ended, Hank had a pretty good stash of music, enough to put out *Songs of
Hank Williams, "The Drifting Cowboy,"* his first WSFA songbook. It included ten uncopyrighted songs and sold for 3 5¢. The book was a matter of
trying out Hank's commercial value. Apparently it proved good enough, for
within a year the *Hank Williams and His Drifting Cowboys, Stars of WSFA,
Deluxe Song Book* was out. This second book offered thirty uncopyrighted
songs, including nine from the first book, and three photos. Hank wrote a
brief preface, thanking his fans and saying that "many of the ideas for
these songs have come from their cards and letters." A second preface, by
WSFA Program Director Caldwell Stewart, describes Hank as being 6 feet
tall and weighing 180 pounds. "He has brown eyes and black hair and a
lazy good-natured air about him. . . . He is happily married and he and 'Miss
Audrey' are already famous as a team."[28] Stewart probably overestimated
Hank's weight and the success of the marriage and the duo.

Most of the songs in these collections are forgettable ditties like "I
Bid You Free to Go" or "Grandad's Musket," the latter a patriotic number

that includes a sharpshooting old man, a grandma who knits socks, and a sister who buys savings stamps. Audrey had gotten her hand into one, a sentimental piece called "My Darling Baby Girl," obviously for Lycrecia. Nothing here yet to get one into the Hall of Fame. But "Honkey-Tonkey" turned up; much later known as "Honky Tonkin'," it practically became the trademark of Hank Williams. And another song should be noted: Apparently, Hank had picked up on Bo Carter's recording of "Back Ache Blues." Maybe the song indicated something of Hank's physical ailment, but certainly it anticipated a lot of good comic tunes—like "Move It on Over" and "Kaw-Liga"—as it tells of being squeezed so hard by a lover that he gets a backache.

The more serious love songs in the collection are the weakest. "I Don't Care (If Tomorrow Never Comes)" offers little to remember as its speaker gives up on life because his girl has left him. "Never Again (Will I Knock on Your Door)" works hard on the theme of lovers who have tried to patch it up too many times. "My Love for You (Has Turned to Hate)" is another song of betrayal; the faithful lover who thought his beloved was true is left behind. "Six More Miles" is a terse piece about seeing a true love to her grave. The two religious songs are startlingly simple. "When God Comes and Gathers His Jewels" depicts a boy, alone and crying, at a graveside. A minister appears to take his hand and predict a reunion in heaven. "Wealth Won't Save Your Soul" is entirely predictable.

No one could get eloquent about the greatness of these songs. But I do think they indicate something important about Hank Williams. The love songs are apparently autobiographical as they speak of lovers like Hank and Audrey who do not seem to be able to get it together and also because they hint at unfaithfulness. The religious songs suggest a pattern in Hank's work. The adult Hank Williams rarely darkened church doors, but he never escaped the religiosity of his childhood. Also, Hank was greatly influenced by Roy Acuff, who knew exactly when to get seriously penitential.[29] Another point concerns the remarkable directness of Hank's work. If most songwriters are busy trying to find unique ways to state the familiar, Hank was content to go straight at it. The threat of a cliche never bothered him; and although this may be counted a weakness, it contributed to the basic honesty that makes his music appealing.

The stash of songs, especially the last six, were going to help Hank make the change of scene that he needed. Montgomery had no music publisher and it certainly had no recording studios. In an earlier day, the big recording outfits had occasionally sent out talent scouts. Victor had found both the Carter family and Jimmie Rodgers on such a trek, but no one came looking for Hank Williams. So it seemed time to head for Nashville and Acuff-Rose, the publisher that dealt primarily with country music.

Hank was provincial, emerging from Alabama for nearly the first time, but Fred Rose had been around. Born in 1897 in Evansville, Indiana, Rose had grown up in St. Louis. Before he drifted south, he had become an accomplished songwriter, author of pieces like "Red Hot Mama" and "Deed I Do." The Fred Rose song best known today, thanks to Willie Nelson, is probably "Blue Eyes Crying in the Rain." He had worked for Fibber McGee and Molly and Paul Whiteman, and he had had his own radio show, "Fred Rose's Song Shop," during which he composed songs on the spot. Rose had even been to Hollywood to do some writing for Gene Autry. That he settled in Nashville, not long before World War II, was to be a blessing for the city itself and for Hank Williams.

As country music grew in popularity, the need for its own house and licensing agency became more and more apparent. The American Society of Composers, Authors, and Publishers (ASCAP), the outfit that collected royalties for public use of songs by its members, paid little attention to country music. The result, as Bill Malone notes in his history of country music, was that "the performance of hillbilly songs was, on the whole, unprotected."[30] ASCAP's contract with the radio networks had expired on 31 December 1940, and the agency wanted to double the price for the next five-year period. The National Association of Broadcasters had seen all of this coming and had established a new licensing company, Broadcast Music, Inc. (BMI), on 14 October 1939. At the beginning of 1941, the broadcasters banned all ASCAP material. BMI was in business, but it needed a stable of writers and songs. The effect was some democracy for the music world: Country music and what is sometimes called "race music" started getting standard copyright protection through BMI, an agency nicely in place for the boom brought to country music by World War II.

Roy Acuff and Fred Rose came to the rescue on the publishing house problem. Acuff, one of the best songwriters of the day and once a gubernatorial candidate in Tennessee, had been having trouble copyrighting his music. So many of his songs had been pirated that he even tried protecting them by writing them on postcards and mailing them to himself in the hope that the postmarks would somehow demonstrate ownership. Acuff had made a small fortune in 1941 when he sold nearly a million copies of a 25¢ fold-out songbook, *Roy Acuff's Folio of Original Songs Featured over WSM Grand Ole Opry*, which could be mailed to fans as a postcard. Thus, music publishing was much on his mind when he met Fred Rose. In October 1942, Acuff gave Rose $25,000 to start Acuff-Rose. Elizabeth Schlappi describes the company:

> Through the years Acuff-Rose has expanded from a tiny firm founded on "a handshake and a promise" to a mammoth corporation which is one of the largest music business complexes in the world and which has played a large part in the growth of country music. From the beginning, Roy Acuff and Fred Rose agreed that the firm would be scrupulously honest and also that it would go out of its way to help deserving talent. Acuff-Rose has done just that—the prime example is Hank Williams.[31]

Hank and Audrey had picked a good time to step off the bus into Nashville. It was 1946, country music was practically everywhere, BMI was on its feet, and good new talent was welcome. Moreover, Hank's long-time idol, Roy Acuff, was in the publishing business now; and Hank's material needed nothing more than the professional hand of Acuff's partner, Fred Rose, a reformed alcoholic, now a Christian Scientist.

Nashville is nearly as full of the mythology of being discovered as Hollywood, and the suicide rate is equally high. Would-be writers can perform a full show of their own compositions; people walk into town with guitars on their backs; and "writer's night," an occasion when anyone is welcome to perform, is a regular club item. One just hopes that the right person will stumble onto his act. Audrey Williams was not so patient; she was not going to wait for her husband's discovery. She took him straight to the best talent promoters in Nashville.

She and Hank showed up at the WSM building at lunchtime on 14 September 1946. Fred Rose, who was looking for some country songs for Molly O'Day, was finishing off the lunch hour with a game of ping-pong with his son, Wesley. Audrey announced that her husband had songs to sing. Fred invited them to a studio, where Hank did several numbers including "My Love for You," "Six More Miles," and "When God Comes and Gathers His Jewels."

One of the myths that intervenes here is that Fred Rose was impressed with the music but was not convinced that Hank had written it. To make Hank prove his claim to the music, Fred gave him a boy-girl plot and asked him to write a song about it then and there. Hank supposedly turned out one of his well-known numbers, "Mansion on the Hill," in thirty minutes. MGM, years later, fell for the tale, and one can see George Hamilton, as an unlikely Hank, write the song in the film *Your Cheatin' Heart.* The source of the myth seems to be Lillie's book, *Our Hank Williams.* Chet Flippo speculates reasonably that the story, long since proven false, was Lillie's attempt to downplay Audrey's part in the discovery of Hank Williams.[32]

Fred Rose, however, was impressed enough to discuss a songwriting contract that would give Hank 3¢ for each copy of sheet music sold and 50 percent of royalties for use of songs by record companies. Supposedly they came to the 3¢ figure when Hank claimed he did not understand how much 3 percent would be, but in reality the contract was a standard one. At any rate, Hank and Audrey headed back to Montgomery. And there, on 31 October, Hank took a sheet of Audrey's printed stationery and wrote Mr. Rose: "Here is the two (2) songs you asked for, and the recordings of them left yesterday. If you can use more at any time, let me know and what type."[33] The manuscripts of "Six More Miles" and "When God Comes and Gathers His Jewels" accompanied the letter. On 21 November, Hank wrote Rose to say that he had received his contract and to "offer 3 or 4 more numbers." Rose responded on 23 November to the effect that the contracts were in order and that Molly O'Day had seen the songs. Rose also noted: "I must change the lyrics around in order to make them consistent. These will be minor changes, and will not interfere with what you have already written." Actually, Rose cut the third stanza of "Six More Miles" and changed a phrase that improved the rhyme of the refrain. The changes in "When God Comes and Gathers His Jewels" were negligible. Molly O'Day was soon to record both songs, and Hank Williams was in the songwriting business.

Before the end of 1946, Hank was back in Nashville and into the recording business. The Roses, who at first saw Hank as only a writer, had gone to Montgomery to see him perform and had come home to look for the chance to record him. In December 1946, Sterling Records called from New York to see if Acuff-Rose could recommend a western band and a country singer for some recording sessions. The Roses thought immediately of a band: The Oklahoma Wranglers, sometimes known as the Willis Brothers, a band consisting of Guy, Vic, and Skeeter Willis. Hank would be the country singer.

Hank did his first session with the Castle Recording Company in Studio D of WSM. As if to forecast part of his destiny, WSM resided in the building of National Life and Accident Insurance Company, the primary sponsor of The Grand Ole Opry. Hank cut his first record there on 11 December 1946; the Oklahoma Wranglers were behind him, with a character known as Chuck "The Indian" on bass. Hank recorded four of his own songs: "Wealth Won't Save Your Soul," "When God Comes and Gathers

His Jewels" (S-204), "Never Again (Will I Knock on Your Door)," and "Calling You" (S-201). All of these sad songs took up lost souls or lost love, subjects Hank understood well.

Sterling liked the cuts, paid Hank a flat $82.50, and invited him back for a second session. On 13 February 1947, a slightly bolder Hank Williams recorded four more songs: "I Don't Care (If Tomorrow Never Comes)," "My Love for You (Has Turned to Hate)" (S-208), "Honky Tonkin'," and "Pan American" (S-210). The first two songs bore the same dreariness of the first records. But "Pan American" and "Honky Tonkin'" were sharp departures from the earlier mournful tone. "Pan American" is an upbeat number about the L&N train that Hank heard whip through Greenville and Georgiana on its way to New Orleans. "Honky Tonkin'," of course, is that rowdy number in which the singer invites somebody else's baby to grab some money and join him in the city.

Hank made another $82.50 and proved that he was not a one-beat performer. Fred Rose liked "Honky Tonkin'" especially and called Frank Walker, a music promoter who had been involved with the careers of singers from Caruso to Al Jolson, Bessie Smith, and Gene Autry. Walker was setting up a recording division of MGM and commissioned Hank's first MGM recording. Hank signed on and pulled out four more compositions for the 21 April 1947 session. "Six More Miles (to the Graveyard)" would back "I Saw the Light" (MGM-10271); the other record (MGM-10033) would package the serious and the bumptious Hank Williams with "Last Night I Heard You Crying in Your Sleep" behind "Move It on Over," the latter a lively number about coming home late, being locked out by an angry wife, and moving in with the family pet. The session was certainly remarkable for a new artist. In fact, John W. Rumble, in his doctoral dissertation on Fred Rose, claims that "Move It on Over" was important in setting MGM Records on "a firm basis."[34] Hank would do two more sessions in the Castle studios before the end of 1947.

All Hank needed now was a good promotional base, something to get those records spinning out into the countryside. He had been doing a six

Figure 8. Hank as a member of the Louisiana Hayride. Photograph courtesy of Bruce Gidoll.

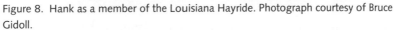

o'clock show every morning in Montgomery, but he was too big for WSFA now and not big enough for The Grand Ole Opry. But The Louisiana Hayride, cranked up by Henry Clay in April 1948, was the right size for Hank's talent. The Hayride convened at Shreveport's Municipal Auditorium, from eight until eleven-thirty every Saturday night. The 50,000 watts of KWKH, managed by Dean Upson, sent it out over western Louisiana and into Texas. The show became a kind of training ground, sometimes known as "the cradle of the stars," for quite a few famous performers, among them George Jones, Webb Pierce, Jim Reeves, Slim Whitman, Kitty Wells, and Faron Young, not to mention Elvis. Hank would be a regular there before the fall.

As one might guess, a good many stories swirl around Hank's entrance to the Hayride. One is that Johnnie Bailes, a Hayride star, found a despondent Hank leaning on a parking meter near the auditorium. When Hank reported that he had been turned down by KWKH, Bailes took him in to insist that he be given a spot on the show. Horace "Hoss" Logan, one of the Hayride producers, reports in his lively memoir, *Elvis, Hank, and Me*, that he had heard Hank's recordings and had invited him to come to Shreveport, provided he would stay sober for six months beforehand, an unlikely prospect.[35] The truth is that Fred Rose had good contacts with the Hayride folk and was almost certainly responsible for Hank's opportunity.

But, as usual, Hank Williams had a domestic crisis to get through first. He and Audrey had been fighting hard—not just a matter of love not running smoothly. The two could get down to blows quickly, and there are many tales of their fights. The situation emphasizes Hank's extremes: Women dominated him easily, and he resented it. Hank was either antagonizing the hell out of Audrey or promoting her career extravagantly, as he had done in his 19 August 1947 letter to Fred Rose: "I sent you the recordings of Audrey and myself yesterday. We did not do much on that 'I Saw the Light' we never had tried it until we went to make the records. Maybe you can get an idea of it. The others are good I think. I also sent that thing—entitled 'Everythings o.K.' Here's hoping you can use the Duet."[36] The problem, no doubt, was Audrey's voice and not the lack of rehearsal that Hank mentions. Sadly ironic is that final line, Hank's recommendation of the duet, which he had just identified as the weakest piece. He had gotten along with Lillie the same way: Hank was either the bad boy stirring trouble or the son eager to make amends.

Audrey had enough of it after about four years of marriage. She left in February 1948 and filed for a divorce, which was granted on 26 May 1948.

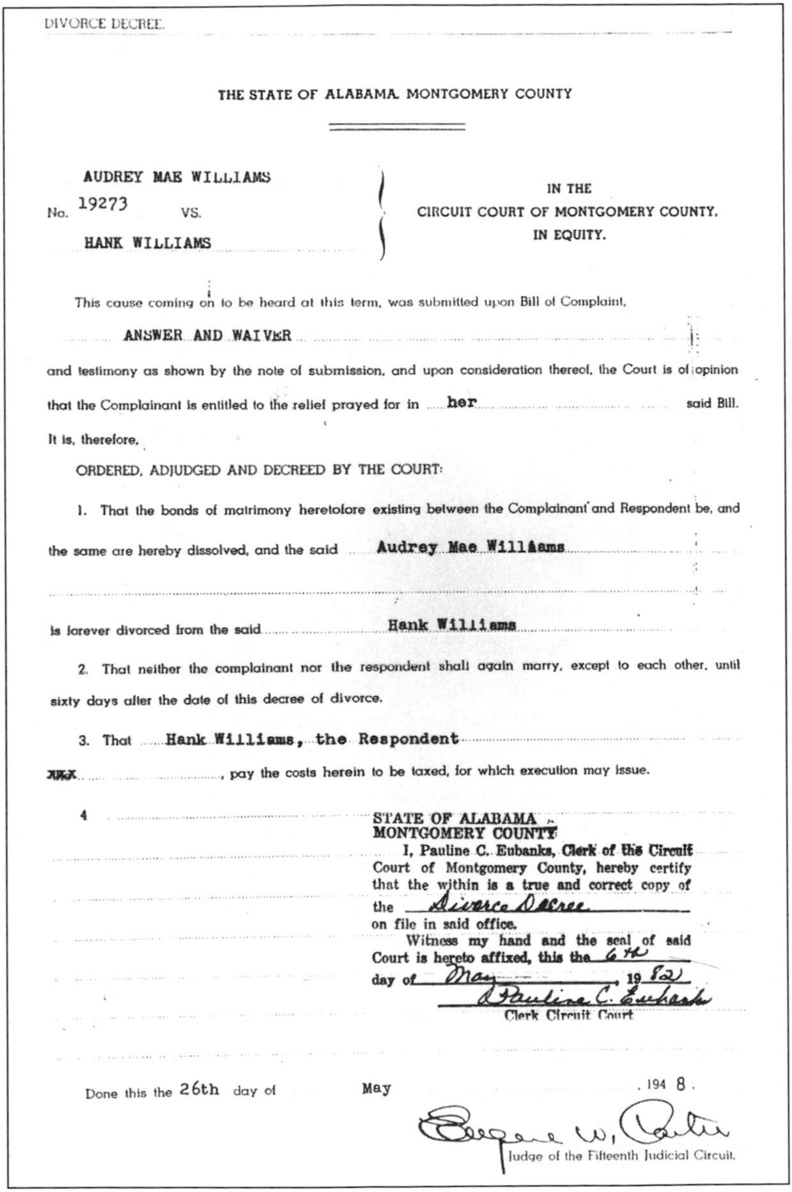

DIVORCE DECREE.

THE STATE OF ALABAMA. MONTGOMERY COUNTY

AUDREY MAE WILLIAMS

No. 19273   VS.

HANK WILLIAMS

IN THE
CIRCUIT COURT OF MONTGOMERY COUNTY.
IN EQUITY.

This cause coming on to be heard at this term, was submitted upon Bill of Complaint,

ANSWER AND WAIVER

and testimony as shown by the note of submission, and upon consideration thereof, the Court is of opinion

that the Complainant is entitled to the relief prayed for in _____ her _____ said Bill.

It is, therefore,

ORDERED, ADJUDGED AND DECREED BY THE COURT:

1. That the bonds of matrimony heretofore existing between the Complainant and Respondent be, and

the same are hereby dissolved, and the said _____ Audrey Mae Williams

is forever divorced from the said _____ Hank Williams

2. That neither the complainant nor the respondent shall again marry, except to each other, until

sixty days after the date of this decree of divorce.

3. That _____ Hank Williams, the Respondent

XXX _____, pay the costs herein to be taxed, for which execution may issue.

4 _____

STATE OF ALABAMA
MONTGOMERY COUNTY
I, Pauline C. Eubanks, Clerk of the Circuit
Court of Montgomery County, hereby certify
that the within is a true and correct copy of
the _____ Divorce Decree _____
on file in said office.
Witness my hand and the seal of said
Court is hereto affixed, this the 6th
day of _____ May _____, 19 82
Pauline C. Eubanks
Clerk Circuit Court

Done this the 26th day of _____ May _____, 194 8 .

Eugene W, Carter
Judge of the Fifteenth Judicial Circuit.

Figure 9. The divorce decree of Hank and Audrey Williams, granted 26 May 1948.

Hank paid the court costs and went back to his drinking.[37] In fact, he went on a real tear, and we might never have heard of him again except for the Hayride offer. He straightened up as well as he could and accepted. Meanwhile, Audrey had come home, and the divorce turned out to be nominal only. Hank and Audrey were traveling together in Norfolk less than a month after the court proceedings, when, on 23 June, not long before the Hayride offer of July, they sent Fred Rose a postcard: "Having Big Time, Hank & Audrey."[38] I am cynical enough to suggest that they were reassuring Fred that, as they worked their way toward the Hayride, life was under control. At any rate, they were on their way to Shreveport, where Hank would debut on the Hayride, with "Move It on Over," on 7 August 1949.

His new routine had him appearing on the Hayride on Saturday nights and doing a daily radio show, sponsored by Johnny Fair Syrup, as the "Old Syrup Sopper." His jingle, "When I die, bury me deep/ in a bucket of Johnny Fair,/ from my head to my feet," is not especially original, but it may have saved a company that was near bankruptcy until Hank Williams showed up. When he was not on the Hayride or at the radio station, he toured the countryside, hitting places like Lake Charles, Texarkana, and Baton Rouge. The towns were just a little bigger than Hank had known in his WSFA days. He had bought a blue, 1948 touring Packard, one big enough to hold his band and pull a trailer. Hank actually drove very little—perhaps because of his weak vision and back problems or because he liked to slouch in the back seat and try to compose a song or two. He had already gotten at least one good song that way. Back in Montgomery, after a long road trip, he had seen the first light of the city and written "I Saw the Light"—or so the story goes.

The Louisiana branch of the Drifting Cowboys was minus Don Helms and Sammy Pruett. Neither of them wanted to move to Shreveport. But Hank gathered a pretty good band, the best known being bass player Lum York and lead guitarist Bob McNett. McNett had been working the Hayride with Patsy Montana. The basic Hank Williams show involved a few numbers by the band to warm up the crowd, the introduction and entrance of Hank, a number by Hank, and then his own personalized, rambling introductions of the individual band members. This was followed by more music and concluded with either a recitation or a sincerely put gospel number, something everyone knew. Hank had done this act out of Montgomery; he would do it again out of Nashville.

He was getting better with audiences. He was handsome, well decked out in a stage uniform that always included a hat to cover his balding head. He seemed unselfconsciously provocative as he hunched over a microphone or gathered himself around a guitar. Logan talks about Hank's hip movements and says "there was something deeply personal and almost sensuous about his delivery...an aura of sexiness that no male country singer ever had before."[39] The Hayride audiences were to see nothing like that again until Elvis showed up. That Hank seemed both aggressive and vulnerable really appealed to the Hayride fans. Maybe it was just Hank Williams, a man whose successes and disasters went hand in hand, coming straight through. Maybe audiences sensed that he knew whereof he spoke, that he had lived a good many of his songs. Whatever the formula, Hank Williams came to life when he hit the stage. In a Roger Williams interview, Frank Page, then producer of the Hayride, says that Hank "was just electrifying on stage...he had the people in the palm of his hands from the moment he walked out there. They were with him, whatever he wanted to do."[40]

Audrey, of course, was still trying to get in on the act. Horace Logan says that occasionally they had to put her on stage, with her mike turned down. He goes on to argue that Audrey's "vain, unrealistic insistence that she be allowed to sing on the same stage with Hank delayed his success and even damaged his career early on."[41] That damage, though, was not apparent. Hank was rolling. He was still drinking—enough to get himself in trouble for pulling down the stage curtain in the middle of a Bailes Brothers act in Lake Charles. And he had to live with the reputation of being a dangerous property, one who might not show or one who might not be en-

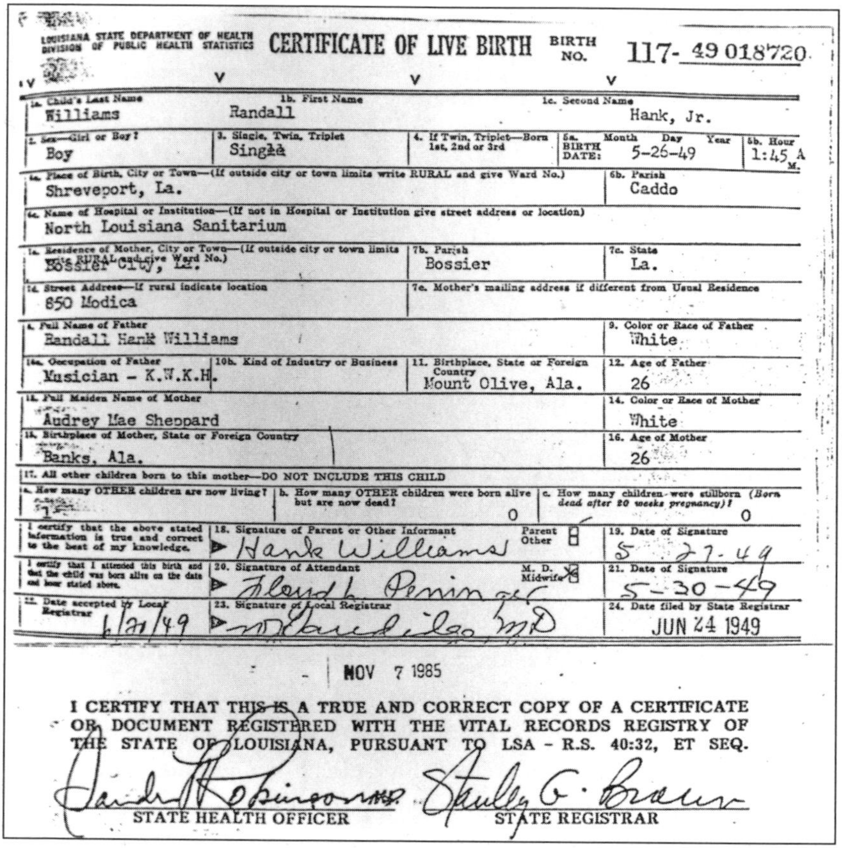

LOUISIANA STATE DEPARTMENT OF HEALTH
DIVISION OF PUBLIC HEALTH STATISTICS
CERTIFICATE OF LIVE BIRTH
BIRTH NO. 117- 49 018720

1a. Child's Last Name: Williams
1b. First Name: Randall
1c. Second Name: Hank, Jr.
2. Sex—Girl or Boy? Boy
3. Single, Twin, Triplet: Single
4. If Twin, Triplet—Born 1st, 2nd or 3rd
5a. BIRTH DATE: Month Day Year 5-26-49
5b. Hour 1:45 A M.
6a. Place of Birth, City or Town—(If outside city or town limits write RURAL and give Ward No.) Shreveport, La.
6b. Parish: Caddo
6c. Name of Hospital or Institution—(If not in Hospital or Institution give street address or location) North Louisiana Sanitarium
7a. Residence of Mother, City or Town—(If outside city or town limits write RURAL and give Ward No.) Bossier City, La.
7b. Parish: Bossier
7c. State: La.
7d. Street Address—If rural indicate location: 850 Modica
7e. Mother's mailing address if different from Usual Residence
8. Full Name of Father: Randall Hank Williams
9. Color or Race of Father: White
10a. Occupation of Father: Musician - K.W.K.H.
10b. Kind of Industry or Business
11. Birthplace, State or Foreign Country: Mount Olive, Ala.
12. Age of Father: 26
13. Full Maiden Name of Mother: Audrey Mae Sheppard
14. Color or Race of Mother: White
15. Birthplace of Mother, State or Foreign Country: Banks, Ala.
16. Age of Mother: 26
17. All other children born to this mother—DO NOT INCLUDE THIS CHILD
a. How many OTHER children are now living? 1
b. How many OTHER children were born alive but are now dead? 0
c. How many children were stillborn (Born dead after 20 weeks pregnancy)? 0
I certify that the above stated information is true and correct to the best of my knowledge.
18. Signature of Parent or Other Informant: Hank Williams — Parent/Other
19. Date of Signature: 5-27-49
I certify that I attended this birth and that the child was born alive on the date and hour stated above.
20. Signature of Attendant: Floyd L. Peninger — M. D./Midwife
21. Date of Signature: 5-30-49
22. Date accepted by Local Registrar: 6/21/49
23. Signature of Local Registrar: [signature], MD
24. Date filed by State Registrar: JUN 24 1949

NOV 7 1985

I CERTIFY THAT THIS IS A TRUE AND CORRECT COPY OF A CERTIFICATE OR DOCUMENT REGISTERED WITH THE VITAL RECORDS REGISTRY OF THE STATE OF LOUISIANA, PURSUANT TO LSA - R.S. 40:32, ET SEQ.

STATE HEALTH OFFICER — STATE REGISTRAR

Figure 10. Hank Jr.'s birth certificate. It indicates that the child was born on 26 May 1949, the first anniversary of his parents' divorce.

tirely in charge of himself when he did show. Audiences, at least at this point, seemed to like the edge, a benefit that a singer like George Jones would enjoy many years later.

At home, Hank could get Audrey stirred up. But the two got cozy enough in the fall of 1948 to conceive Randall Hank Williams, known today as Hank Williams Jr.[42] During Audrey's confinement, Hank got a big break.

He recorded a song called "The Lovesick Blues" at the Herzog Studio in Cincinnati on 22 December 1948. The record (MGM-10352) was released in February 1949. The song was not his; Irving Mills and Cliff Friend had copyrighted it in 1922. It had been recorded by Emmett Miller and Rex Griffin. Hank had been playing it for some time, making the song more or less his own with a jaunty yodeling despair that he could do better than anyone.

The song was a wild hit. *Billboard* was to list it as the number one country and western record of 1949, and *Cash Box* voted it the "Best Hillbilly Record" of the year. Songs like George Morgan's "Candy Kisses," Red Foley's "Tennessee Border," and Eddie Arnold's "Bouquet of Roses" provided "The Lovesick Blues" with some good competition that year. The content of the song clearly fit this singer, and the huge success left Hank with a new nickname: He became "The Lovesick Blues Boy" or just "Lovesick" among his friends who were joshing him about both his personal and his professional lives. So old "Lovesick" Hank Williams became the number two man in *Billboard*'s top selling folk artist category that year. A fine irony is that the rating got a slight boost from another Hank Williams hit: "Wedding Bells" (MGM-10401) had made it to number five on the 1949 charts.

The problem now belonged to The Grand Ole Opry and its officials, Harry Stone and Jim Denny. The Opry has always successfully cultivated a family image. Country music lovers come from everywhere to see the show, and they behave remarkably well. Stone and Denny knew about Hank's affection for whiskey, and they knew there might be something a little lascivious about the way he went at a love song. They were frightened of him, yet his "Lovesick Blues," one of the best records spinning, could not be ignored. Their solution was to offer Hank a guest appearance.

Introduced by Red Foley, Hank appeared for the first time on The Grand Ole Opry on 11 June 1949. The audience's response to his coming on stage was slight. Not everyone knew exactly who Hank Williams was, but everybody knew "Lovesick Blues." Before the twenty-five-year-old singer could get through a few bars, the crowd of more than 3,500 was up off of the hard oak pews that served as seats in Ryman Auditorium. They called him back to the stage six times.

All Hank had to do was accept the now-inevitable Opry contract and put together a good band so he could get on the road, just as he had done in Shreveport, except now it was for much more money. Before coming to Nashville, he had dismissed his Hayride band, which some see as reflecting Hank's confidence in being through with the minor leagues. He caught up with Don Helms, one of the Drifting Cowboys who had not been willing to move to Shreveport. Don was certainly interested in Nashville and the Opry, and he rejoined the band. Bob McNett came up from Shreveport. Jerry Rivers, who had declined at least one earlier offer, agreed to be fiddler. Hillous Butrum, a twenty-one-year-old who had been an Opry sideman for five years, signed on as bass player. Hank was set. They went on the road so fast that several members of the band had to borrow the appropriate western clothing.

At the same time, and as usual, Hank had to deal with his domestic situation, and it was a little more complicated than it had been. Randall Hank had been born just sixteen days before Hank had opened on the Opry. Maybe he was trying to assure Fred Rose that his life was conventional; but certainly Hank sounded like the proud dad when, on 26 May 1949, the first anniversary of his divorce from Audrey, he wired Mr. and Mrs. Fred Rose from Shreveport: "10 lb boy borned this morning at 1:45 Both doeing fine."[43] Hank nicknamed the boy "Bocephus," after a puppet used by Opry comedian Rod Brasfield. And he took to closing his radio shows with his usual "If the good Lord's willing and the creek don't rise, we'll be back for another visit," but now with the addition, "See you in a little while Bocephus," or "I'm coming, Bocephus."

He sounded like the good family man, anxious to get off the air and on the road back to the hearth, just the right thing for Opry fans. Apparently, however, Hank really was good with the children. Lycrecia, who had left

Montgomery in 1948 to return to live with Audrey's parents, was back as part of the Nashville household. In her memoir, *Still in Love with You*, she shows much affection for Hank, more than she shows for Audrey. She explains that Hank never legally adopted her only because Audrey "was afraid that he would take me away from her if they ever divorced."[44] Hank's gifts for the children were famously extravagant, horses for Lycrecia and cowboy suits and boots for Hank Jr. He might have been remembering his own fatherless childhood, and I suspect he was enjoying the idea that he really did have a family.

At any rate, the summer of 1949 was intense: The birth of Hank Jr., the Opry debut, and the move to Nashville cluttered the busy performing schedule. Plus, Hank and Audrey had some more legal work to do. Whether they were tidying things up for the charge at the Opry or just being decent parents, they started taking care of the 1948 divorce. They had it amended *nunc pro tunc* on 9 August 1949, which left the original decree meaningless because it eliminated all three of its points, particularly the one stating that "Audrey Mae Williams is forever divorced from the said Hank Williams." The document states that this action seems to be "in the best interest of both petitioners and of their minor son, Randall Hank Williams."[45] Hank and Audrey were man and wife once more.

Audrey was pleased enough about the document and about living in Nashville. She wanted Hank to be successful, but she did crave a larger part in that success. Even if no one else noticed, she was certainly aware of her absence at the 11 June Opry performance. Audrey was probably changing a diaper in Louisiana while Hank was taking his six encores, and little Hank would continue to keep her out of action for a while. When she was finally ready to return to what she imagined as her singing career, her husband did not have much room for her on stage. It might have been easy enough to give her a bit in an Alabama honky-tonk five years before or even to set her up with a nearly silent mike on the Louisiana Hayride. But she had not been a part of the breakthrough into the big time. At the Opry, the

AUDREY MAE WILLIAMS,

        COMPLAINANT   IN THE CIRCUIT COURT OF MONTGOMERY

    VS.   COUNTY, ALABAMA

HANK WILLIAMS,   IN EQUITY

        RESPONDENT

This cause coming on to be heard on the sworn bill filed by Audrey Mae Williams and Hank Williams and upon supporting affidavits filed by both of the parties, and it appearing to the court that there is no party adversely interested in the relief prayed for and that it will be in the best interest of both petitioners and of their minor son, Randall Hank Williams, that the relief prayed for be granted.

It is therefore ordered, adjudged and decreed by the court that the decree in this cause rendered on the 26th day of May, 1948 be and the same is hereby amended nunc pro tunc by striking from said decree the following paragraphs:

1. That the bonds of matrimony heretofore existing between the Complainant and Respondent be and the same are hereby dissolved and the said Audrey Mae Williams is forever divorced from the said Hank Williams.

2. That neither the Complainant nor the Respondent shall again marry except to each other until sixty days after the date of this decree of divorce.

3. That Hank Williams, the Respondent, pay the costs herein to be taxed for which execution may issue.

And further, by striking from the decree the court's finding that the Complainant is entitled to the relief prayed for in her original bill and substituting therefor a finding that the Complainant is not entitled to the relief prayed for in her original bill; further, that the decree shall read, as amended, that the Complainant's bill of complaint be dismissed and that the costs of said proceeding be paid by the Respondent Hank Williams.

It is further ordered, adjudged and decreed by the court that Hank Williams pay the costs herein to be taxed for which execution may issue.

Done this the 9 day of August, 1949.

STATE OF ALABAMA
MONTGOMERY COUNTY
I, Pauline C. Eubanks, Clerk of the Circuit Court of Montgomery County, hereby certify that the within is a true and correct copy of the *Decree Amending Divorce Decree of May 26, 1948 Nunc Pro Tunc* on file in said office. Witness my hand and the seal of said Court is hereto affixed, this the 6th day of May, 1982.

                                       Eugene W. Carter
                                       Circuit Judge

Pauline C. Eubanks
Clerk Circuit Court

Figure 11. These amendments to the 1948 divorce of Hank and Audrey, filed on 9 August 1949, eliminated all of the terms of the divorce.

act was Hank Williams and the Drifting Cowboys, not Mr. and Mrs. Williams the duo. This would be a continuing problem for Hank and Audrey.

Hank's constant travel did not help the relationship either because it allowed personal jealousies to grow along with the professional one. The legally reunited couple would get back to the usual fighting, probably with more alcohol thrown into the bargain. When Audrey accused him of infidelity, Hank returned the favor; trust never found a way into the marriage, and failure at home again undercut the success of Hank Williams. The marriage would be no match for the crises that lay ahead.

The Grand Ole Opry worked like the Hayride; WSM served the same function as KWKH and, for that matter, WSFA. But the Opry was the central point for country music. The stars performed there on Saturday night, for union scale, and then hit the road for better money in the places where they had been heard courtesy of WSM. They returned to Ryman Auditorium for the Saturday shows, or at least for the twenty-six shows called for in the standard contract. Hank knew the cycle well—it was making him famous and killing him all at once.

In recounting his days as a Drifting Cowboy, Jerry Rivers is especially nostalgic about the first part of Hank's stay in Nashville:

> The days from 1949 till 1951 were some of the best times of my life.... This was the period when Hank Williams made the fastest rise in popularity, wrote his best songs, and probably helped advance country music further than in any previous decade. During this time Hank's health was good, his attitude and enthusiasm were at an all-time high and no one ever gained the professional respect and acceptance of the industry so rapidly.[46]

Rivers's enthusiasm here was fair enough; this *was* by far the best part of the career of Hank Williams. The *Billboard* summary of recordings with the best retail sales for 1950 included three of his numbers: "Why Don't You Love Me?" (4), "Long Gone Lonesome Blues" (5), and "Moanin' the Blues" (30). The year 1951 would bring "Cold, Cold Heart" (1), "Hey Good Lookin'" (8), and "Crazy Heart" (29).

Figure 12. The Drifting Cowboys and their families at Hank's home on Franklin Road in Nashville. From left to right: Bob McNett, Hank, Audrey, Hank Jr., Lycrecia, Hazel Helms, Frankie Helms, June Rivers, Don Helms, Betty Butrum, Hillous Butrum (standing), and Jerry Rivers. Photograph courtesy of Bruce Gidoll.

Hank and the Cowboys took advantage of their currency. They played in every kind of setting—from civic auditoriums to the rooftops of drive-in movie snack bars—and they worked hard on stage. Hank and the band often had to do entire shows. Sometimes a comedian was thrown in and occasionally another unit joined, but basically Hank and the Cowboys carried the load. Thus, the group had to be versatile. A bass player like Hillous Butrum, called "Buel" on stage, had to play, sing, and tell jokes. All were counted on for the stage chatter that may be responsible for a good bit of the corniness associated with country music. Hank carried on a standard set of jokes with the band. Jerry Rivers was "Burrhead" because of his closely cut blond hair, and he was the object of newlywed jokes long after his 1949 marriage. Bob McNett had to go by his full name, Rupert Robert McNett, in Hank's introductions. Because he was a native of Pennsylvania, he had to put up with Hank's long string of North-South jokes. Don Helms performed as "Shag," and Hank had to go by the name "Harm," a countrified version of the already countrified Hiram.

Bob Pinson, head of acquisitions at The Country Music Foundation Library and Media Center in Nashville and one of country music's best scholars, described for me a typical itinerary, this one from 1950: "On August 12 Hank performed on the Opry. On August 13, he was in Springfield, Ohio. On the 14th, it was Youngstown, Ohio. Then Akron on the 15th and probably New Lewiston, Pennsylvania, on the 16th. On the 17th, he appeared in Richmond, Virginia. And he most likely appeared somewhere else on the 18th before returning to Nashville for the Opry on the 19th. The schedule could be very grueling."[47]

When possible, Hank pulled into a local radio station for a quick interview plugging his work. When he headed south, he liked to stop at WRFS, in Alexander City, Alabama, to visit Bob McKinnon, a popular disc jockey who became an authority on Hank's life. In a 1950 interview, McKinnon tries hard to get on to the promotion of "Long Gone Lonesome Blues," but Hank steadily refers things to Audrey, who he calls his "War Department." When he asked Hank what new recordings were coming up, McKinnon got this answer:

HANK: I don't know what's comin' up next. They don't tell me. Everybody else finds out before I do. By the way, Audrey's gonna make some records here a little later. They talkin' to her about recording. She's gonna record for Decca. You ought to have some of them before long.

McKINNON: I sure do, ah, ah...I'm gonna look for 'em, Hank. I don't have any of 'em now. But...

HANK: They haven't made 'em yet.

McKINNON: Maybe that's why I haven't got any.

HANK: That's possible.

MCKINNON: How was this overseas trip you took here a while back?

HANK: Aw, that was a fine deal. We went to...we went to Berlin, we went to Vienna, we went to Wiesbaden [Hank is very careful with the pronunciation, which brings a good bit of laughter] we strictly went to Wiesbaden. We went all over the occupied zone over there. Where we had any boys at all we went to see 'em. And by the way, on the nineteenth, me and the boys are goin' to Alaska and see all the boys up there, gonna go up and pick them a few tunes, that is, if we can get thawed out enough.[48]

Indeed, Hank was in good spirits here on his home turf. But even near the top of his fame, he was trying hard to promote records his wife had not yet cut instead of his own big hit. To me, he seems to be wishing her a career with Decca, a career, perhaps, independent of his own. I might note that Audrey was present for this interview.

Hank and the Cowboys still traveled in the 1948 Packard, with loud speakers on top and the musicians and instruments jammed inside. The small aluminum trailer they pulled was hard on the car's brakes and had to be abandoned. The car had no power equipment, no air conditioning. It was a tough assignment to drive from Nashville on a Sunday morning after an Opry show, up into the outback of West Virginia or Ohio or down through Carolina for a one-shot performance at a drive-in movie. The crew, though, was young and resilient, and their travels produced many good on-the-road stories. Jerry Rivers's book, *Hank Williams: From Life to Legend,* is the best source of these tales. Exploding cigarette loads were a popular joke, especially because Hank was so bad about bumming smokes and was brazen enough simply to fish them out of someone else's pocket. A newfangled window air conditioner, which was desperately needed down through Louisiana, dumped its several gallons of water on Hank, who then smashed it on the roadside. They hit a buzzard, which came through the windshield and spread itself generously throughout the car. Shag Helms supposedly helped Hank with "I Can't Help It (If I'm Still in Love with You)," which concerns passing an old lover on the street. Shag supplied the rhyme, "And

I smelled your rotten feet." Hank kept writing, at least when he was not trying to keep up with two or three baseball games on the Packard's radio.

Even these happy trips, though, had their problems—when Hank got into his cups. Don Helms told me that Hank was a binge drinker who would "just go until he got nasty. . . . For five or six days, sometimes eight or ten, boy would he drink, just stay wiped out, till we put him in to dry out." Thus, according to Helms, Hank ended more than one tour by returning not to Franklin Road but to Nashville's Madison Sanitarium. Don described an instance for me:

> He'd fight on the way. He called it "The Hut." They had some little outbuild- ings with bars on the windows, special dry-out tanks. One time we brought him in off the road; he did not know where we were going. We pulled up and said "Come on, Hank; let's get out." And he said, "Oh no, oh no, I ain't goin' in there; that's that fucking hut." The attendants would get him in there and he'd sit and look at us like, "Well, you have screwed me again." He'd stay in three or four days, sometimes a week. I'd take him candy bars and comic books every day and check on him. I lived pretty close. About the third day he would perk up and say, "Reckon when they gonna let us out of here?"[49]

Despite such episodes Hank was included in the first Grand Ole Opry/R. J. Reynolds Tobacco Company Tour of U.S. military bases abroad, which be- gan 13 November 1949. Stars like Roy Acuff, Red Foley, Minnie Pearl, and Jimmy Dickens were his colleagues. The company was fast, but Hank held his own easily with "Lovesick Blues," which was as popular with the sol- diers in Germany as it was stateside. The Drifting Cowboys did not make the trip, but Audrey did. Both Jimmy Dickens and Minnie Pearl recalled for Roger Williams that the trip went well enough for Hank as performer and as husband.[50]

Whatever the status of Hank and Audrey's romance, the cash and atten- tion were booming. Hank was doing a Saturday afternoon show for Duck- head Work Clothes, and he was touring constantly, even into Canada. In

1949, he was getting $250 a show; the price went to $1,000 for 1950. He could afford the $40,000 home back in Nashville at 4916 Franklin Road, near the governor's mansion. Eventually the house was to have a wrought iron fence with the notes of "Lovesick Blues" cast in it. And soon Hank was buying a 500 acre farm on Carter's Creek in Franklin, just outside of Nashville. He was going to hunt and ride there, maybe restore the old house, and generally lead the life of country music success. He bought himself a new green 1950 Cadillac. And to keep things more or less even on Franklin Road, he bought Audrey a yellow 1949 Cadillac convertible, with a platinum watch and a diamond ring thrown in for good measure. Some still swear that Hank Williams would take both cars on his visits to Montgomery.

He was well enough off that, although the band drove, he could fly to the West Coast for several shows in 1950. Henry Cannon, Minnie Pearl's husband, was usually the private pilot. In Sacramento, Fresno, San Jose, and Long Beach, Hank and the Cowboys played before the large crowds that were turning out to hear the eight- to twelve-piece western swing bands that were popular in the huge ballrooms, in places like Tex Williams's Riverside Rancho, Spade Cooley's Santa Monica Ballroom, and Smokey Rogers's Bostonia Ballroom. That a five-piece, hard country band could carry a show for 2,000 patrons who were accustomed to the swing orchestras is remarkable testimony to the skill and popularity of Hank Williams and the Drifting Cowboys. Hank was well enough known that he took an alias, Herman P. Willis, when he went to Dallas to work for Jack Ruby in July 1950. The band thought he had ducked out on them until they spotted him in their hotel lobby. Hank appointed Jerry Rivers head of the group for the rest of the trip, and he had the following statement notarized on 5 July: "This is to certify that Jerry M. Rivers is the General Manager of Hank Williams & Band. Including Hank Williams. During my stay in State of Texas. Hank Williams."[51] Whether he was getting ready for some serious drinking or was in need of anonymity for other reasons, the celebrity was lying low.

His record sales went over 1 million in 1950; for that year and the next, his releases averaged 500,000 sales each. He got Sam Hunt, a vice president of Nashville's Third National Bank, to help with his money. But Hank bothered little with the sophisticated investments that we associate with superstars today. He was a cash man who supposedly came off the road and into the bank lugging bills and checks that he had not even counted, telling the cashiers that if he could make it, they could count it. Supposedly, he once took $5,000 in small bills to toss around and roll in at home.

Hank did have a few small schemes to turn some extra cash. He started recording some rather moralistic recitations under the name of "Luke the Drifter." Hank seemed to enjoy the melodrama of Luke's pronouncements about life in numbers like "Pictures from Life's Other Side," which shows the tragedy of fallen lives, "Too Many Parties and Too Many Pals," which does the same, "The Funeral," which uses the burial of a black child to make a point about God loving all, and "Be Careful of Stones That You Throw." Roy Acuff had written "Advice to Joe," a number warning Stalin about his soul, and Luke and Fred Rose were ready to follow up with a bouncy recitation called "No, No, Joe," which identified a place in hell for the dictator. Hank, basically known as a honky-tonker, found a second image in Luke. Those who ran the jukebox concessions would take everything by Hank but skip anything by Luke because the latter was more suitable for radio and retail sales than for the juke joints. Hank cut his first two "Luke" sides on 10 January 1950 (MGM-10718) and would go on to do a dozen more.

In 1951, Hank and Jimmy Rule, a math teacher in a private Nashville school who moonlighted as a songwriter, put out a small book called *How to Write Folk and Western Music to Sell*. The book could be ordered from Nashville's Harpeth Publishing Company for $1, postage paid. The advice was reasonable, if ordinary: Get a good title; remember the basic types of songs, for example, those about love, the novelties (like "Rag Mop"), and the "Chamber of Commerce" songs (like "Tennessee Waltz"); keep a notebook; work with 4/4 time; keep it clean; and watch out for song sharks (that is, never pay to have a song published).

Hank's other gesture toward the financial world came in 1951, when he and Audrey opened a western wear store, Hank and Audrey's Corral, in downtown Nashville on Commerce Street. The impression, however, is that this was less an investment and more Audrey keeping up the pace of fame in a town where stars are involved in selling everything from records and cowboy boots to fried chicken. Chet Flippo says that the place was "decorated in true Audrey style. The outside was fake-log cabin, there was a big wagon wheel lamp hanging over the entrance, and there was a big neon sign with pictures of Hank and Audrey on it."[52] WSM broadcast the opening, and Hank, Audrey, Big Bill Lister, and the Drifting Cowboys performed. The crowds must have been impressed both by the hoopla and by the Hank—and Audrey—dolls that were for sale.

Music, though, was the main business of Hank Williams, and music was the source of his money. He had to revise his band somewhat. Much against Hank's wishes, Bob McNett had left in May 1950 to open a country music park in Pennsylvania. Sammy Pruett, who had been playing in Birmingham as one of Happy Wilson's Golden River Boys, rejoined the group as McNett's replacement. In July, Hillous Butrum left to join Hank Snow's band. Howard Watts, the bass player well known as "Cedric Rainwater," left Lester Flatt and Earl Scruggs to replace Butrum. The band was as good as ever, and so was business.

Hank's songs were even spreading into pop, a rare accomplishment for country music at that time. Polly Bergen recorded "Honky Tonkin'." And then, in 1951, Mitch Miller assigned "Cold, Cold Heart," which Hank had recorded in 1950, to Tony Bennett. The Bennett version was the number one song of the year, a million seller that stayed on the charts for forty-six weeks. Supposedly, Hank could hardly get past a jukebox without stopping to hear Bennett do his number. Jerry Rivers explains Hank's fascination with the Bennett recording: "Hank Williams usually recorded with five musicians and played his own open rhythm guitar, used no drums and only occasional light piano for rhythm.... You can imagine the thrill it was to Hank when Tony Bennett recorded 'Cold, Cold Heart' with the full Hollywood treatment."[53] Hank might also have been thrilled at the thought of the fees BMI was collecting for him each time the record played. He must have been just as pleased to find that Joni James, Frankie Laine, Jo Stafford, and Rosemary Clooney were quick to get to his music.

Late in the summer of 1951, Hank got involved in a show put on by a wild-eyed Cajun, Dudley "Couzain Dud" LeBlanc. Described by one historian as a "mercurio-politico," Dudley had run for governor of Louisiana in 1932. His campaign slogan, "the state needs an honest man and I must make the sacrifice," did not carry him into office.[54] And he had to be content with a smaller life as president pro tempore of the state senate and as quack inventor. He had come up with Happy Day Headache Powders and Dixie Dew Cough Remedy, but his greatest accomplishment was Hadacol, a murky patent medicine that was certainly 12 percent alcohol and probably 88 percent swamp water. Hadacol was a big hit across the dry American South, where the belt of a good cocktail, delivered in the guise of medicine, was more than welcome. Dudley promoted it as being especially good for one's sex life, and Hadacol jokes flourished. One concerned a thin, exhausted man who goes to the doctor and says that his problem might be the Hadacol. When the doctor tells him to quit taking it, he responds, "It ain't me that's taking it, it's my wife." Another joke concerned a woman who could not sleep because of her husband's snoring, so she started drinking a bottle every night. She wrote to thank Couzain Dud, saying that now she could sleep with anyone.

Dudley's great marketing trick was the Hadacol Caravan, a traveling show of well-known performers. He would schedule the show in an area that was not blessed with his medicine and announce that admission would be the box top from his product—the box top, of course, completely refundable if the show did not please. The citizenry would besiege the drug stores that had no Hadacol, and then Dudley's salesmen would arrive to supply the grog in the nick of time.

Figure 13. The Hadacol Caravan. Hank is standing in the top left corner, and Candy Candido is second from Hank's left. Photograph courtesy of Marie Harvell.

Dudley had pulled this off very well in 1950, but he had a bad habit of overextending himself and getting into tax trouble. By the middle of 1951, he had serious problems and was ready to sell the company. To give it the air of prosperity, Dudley organized another caravan. This tour was to start in New Iberia, Louisiana and travel several southern states and then move on to Ohio, Indiana, Kansas, and Texas. The show traveled by private train, seventeen cars' worth, and was to make forty-nine one-night stops. LeBlanc assembled a corps of acts including some circus groups as well as performers like Tony Martin, Candy Candido, Carmen Miranda, Dick Haymes, Jack Dempsey, and Hank Williams and the Drifting Cowboys. Stars like Bob Hope and Milton Berle had contracts for a few of the shows and flew in to perform. Dudley, of course, showed up to campaign the Louisiana stops.

The tour got started on 15 August 1951, and the fun was on for Hank and the boys. The circumstances were plush—no driving, good food, free cleaning, and no end of pretty girls. The lovelies included a corps of dancers from Chicago's Chez Paree and ten Hadacol Queens, who, for better or worse, had won the tour in regional beauty contests. The main thing, though, was that Hank and the Drifting Cowboys were running with major stars, not just country ones. Indeed, in many instances, they found themselves more popular than the better known figures. Jerry Rivers told me in an interview that, at this point, it was becoming even clearer that Hank and the band really were a major attraction.[55]

The episode that illustrates that point best concerns one of two performances in Louisville. Bob Hope arrived to close out the program. Hank, who had been closing for Hadacol, preceded Hope. He did "Lovesick Blues" that night. Even after three encores, the crowd was still so wild over him that Hope could not get recognized on stage. Finally, Hope put on a cowboy hat and went out to introduce himself as "Hank Hope." After the show, he made it plain that he did not intend to follow Hank Williams again.

In another incident, this one in Kansas City, Hank stood his ground with Milton Berle. Supposedly, Berle had been trying to run off a photographer backstage until Hank intervened on behalf of the photographer. During the show, Berle was being a ham and upstaging Dick Haymes's performance of "Old Man River." Hank, the story goes, sent word to Berle that he would crack his skull with a guitar if he did not behave. Berle withdrew, and Hank took his place at the end of the show.

The point is not to argue that Hank Williams was more talented than comedian Bob Hope or tougher than Milton Berle or that any of them was a bigger attraction than the other. The comparisons do not get very far in any case because the Hadacol crowd might have been much more the audience of Hank Williams than of the others. But what we do see here is Hank holding forth with some really major stars, just as he had done on the tour of Germany two years before. Both tours, the one for R. J. Reynolds and the other for Hadacol, indicated the growing status of country music as well as that of Hank Williams.

Hank was pleased with all of it. He had proved his appeal, and he had behaved fairly well. He did not seem especially upset when the Hadacol Caravan disbanded in Dallas after only thirty-four shows. Dudley had claimed that he was selling the company for $8 million, but the sale and the company went down the drain when the government placed a tax lien of $665,000 and the Federal Trade Commission filed a complaint of "false, misleading, and deceptive advertising" against Hadacol. Some believe that the performers did not even get paid. Hank was supposed to be getting $1,000 a week plus his expenses, but one story is that only Bob Hope got paid. Jerry Rivers discounted that story in a letter to me dated 25 March 1982:

Hank and Minnie [Pearl] had a "wedge" not available to all the artists. Most every Saturday they would fly in to the Opry in Nashville, and they would leave word that they would not return unless they were paid in full to date. Don [Helms] seems to recall that Hank may have been out a thousand or two for some of the last dates before the collapse of the tour. Furthermore, I would question that superstars such as Milton Berle, Jimmy Durante, Jack Benny, Bob

Hope, etc. would perform without advance deposit and likely full pay prior to performance time. More than likely, those artists who were "hungry" for the work were the ones who got shafted.

Paid in full or not, a confident Hank Williams was on his way back to Nashville in Henry Cannon's Beechcraft Bonanza on 18 September.

Hank even got a chance at Hollywood, one that he missed. Joe Pasternak offered him a bit part as sheriff with Jane Powell and Farley Granger in *Small Town Girl.* When Hank turned it down, MGM came through with a better offer. Jerry Rivers says it was worth about $5,000 a week.[56] The next step was to go to Hollywood to meet Dore Schary. No one says much about what happened. Apparently, Hank was surly and, according to one source, put his feet on Schary's desk and refused to take off his hat. But I suspect that Schary could contend with such minor problems. Wesley Rose says that in addition to the above discourtesies, Hank had "otherwise acted disrespectful."[57] My suspicion is that Hank misbehaved so broadly that even Hollywood marked him as an undependable property. He came home empty-handed, and MGM was later to deny that a contract had ever been issued.

Hank was in better form for a couple of television appearances, one on *The Perry Como Show* and another on *The Kate Smith Evening Hour.* A kinescope of the latter is available at The Country Music Foundation Library and Media Center in Nashville. Hank sang "Hey, Good Lookin'" on this 1952 program, and he did a decent job—although he looked gaunt and hollow-eyed. He did not do as well on his trip to Las Vegas. The place had seen the likes of Rex Allen and Judy Canova, but it was unfamiliar with really hard country music. Hank did not further Nashville's cause any. He was drinking heavily, and at the insistence of Jim Denny, Jerry Rivers and Don Helms had driven him to Nevada, thus giving him time to dry out some. Even so, Hank was not in very good shape when he hit the stage of the Last Frontier Casino. Hard country was going to be awhile getting back to Vegas, partly because of Hank and partly because its fans were not high rollers at the gambling tables. Hank was never going back. The episode was just one more fumbled opportunity.

THE END

A neat chronology of the rise and fall of Hank Williams is impossible, just as impossible as giving a firm explanation of what did him in. We might like to see him thriving through 1951 and then declining as fame got the best of the country boy or as his back problem and marriage grew worse. All of these were factors; but Hank was a committed drinker on his own, and the various problems of his life only intensified a long-time bad habit.

He had grown up in a hard-drinking world. Hank's cousin J. C. McNeil explained to me that drink was a matter of course with Hank and several of his cousins. For many years, J. C. matched Hank drink for drink. He says they were binge drinkers who did not go at it "just for a day or two but until it was gone." And he says that his own survival resulted from an understanding family who took care of him when he was drinking, a family that eventually led him away from drink. Hank had no such benefit. Lillie almost always gave him a bad time when he was on a binge, and she was quick to put him in St. Jude's Hospital in Montgomery with a "No Visitors" sign. Audrey would almost always go home to her family when Hank mentioned whiskey. Occasionally, Hank would turn up at his father's place in McWilliams, and sometimes one of the McNeil brothers would help take care of him. But he was usually on his own when he was hitting the bottle.

Nashville was not much help. Indeed, something can be said for the idea that Hank was really a country boy fallen into that town's fast living. He never deserted his rural ways and never seems to have had such an intention. He was comfortable around only the people he knew very well, most of them relatives or members of the band. He visited cousins like Taft and Erleen Skipper faithfully and, according to J. C. McNeil, had no trouble returning to his origins even after fame had set in. He became especially fond of Lon Williams, as if he were trying to recapture a lost father, and he was true to friends like Braxton and Ola Schuffert.

But he had trouble with the city and the success it represented to him. Nashville's basic response was to try to keep Hank on his feet and to keep his problems away from his fans. It seemed to have no long-term treatment for him. As already indicated, Hank built none of the financial empires expected of stars; he made his cash, as he had done shining shoes and delivering groceries, and he and Audrey spent it. He was not smooth socially. The dinner party circuit was not for Hank, either because he drank too much or because he put ketchup on practically everything he ate. His grammar was bad, as witnessed by the letters already cited. Also, he had a thick, rural accent: "picture" was "pitcher," "hired" was "hard," and "Canada" was "Canader," for example.

Hank read little except comic books, which he self-consciously called "goof" books, and the *Billboard* charts that he could produce from his wallet in a flash. He clung to his hunting and fishing, but did not go into the big-time versions of the sport. He liked to ride his horse Highlife out on the Franklin farm. Tennis and golf must have struck him as a little strange and fraudulent, if they struck him at all; bowling was sophisticated enough for Hank. He collected guns and continued to carry one, a habit that startled quite a few, particularly when he was taking his drink seriously.

Nashville is not inept at accommodating this kind of man. Good old boys and rowdy ways can still flourish there in spite of the more or less cosmopolitan urges of the city and its music business. But being rough around the edges created a problem for Hank at home. Audrey, as homespun as Hank, had social ambitions. She wanted the house on Franklin Road, and she was responsible for eventually expanding the three-bedroom, two-bath place to some 14,000 square feet, including seven bedrooms, six and a half baths, a ballroom, and a Polynesian garden with pool. She was to design an all white "angel" room for herself, along with a bar covered with hearts. Audrey wanted the store on Commerce Street, the clothes, and the social life that came with the success she had helped accumulate for her husband. One can imagine Hank coming in off the road or emerging from "The Hut" to find one more strange Audrey application of the money.

The conflict of styles was not their only problem. Hank did not help the marriage by singing "Cold, Cold Heart" and "Your Cheatin' Heart" with so much plain conviction. Fans had a good idea by now of who he was singing about. And Hank and Audrey fought over who was responsible for his success. The talent was obviously his, but she had sold him to the Roses. Women were also a problem; they flocked to Hank, and he found them hard to resist. Taft Skipper, Hank's cousin, told me that the men in the family were always bad about that. Heredity or not, Hank's womanizing certainly brought down the wrath of Miss Audrey; and Hank seemed to have trouble handling the guilt that came with his affairs. Audrey was quick to get even with him, and she returned the unfaithfulness. Her affairs fueled Nashville gossip throughout her life there. They tortured Hank, especially on the road where he did his hardest drinking. Sometimes he would phone her over and over, finding her out. Then he would drink harder until he returned to Nashville for either a stint at Madison Sanitarium or a major fight there on Franklin Road. At least one of those fights would include some gunfire, another found Hank breaking out a storm door with his guitar, and another involved his throwing her new wardrobe into the yard.

A basic element of Hank's personality is probably confirmed in his domestic mess, his infidelities, and the effect of Audrey's infidelities. Hank, from beginning to end, was insecure. His case is classic, a Nashville version of what happened to people like Marilyn Monroe in Hollywood. He came out of a shaky family. His father was gone for most of his childhood, and moving was nearly an annual event. He went from a domineering mother to a domineering wife; and he won fame and success that he did not altogether understand, that he was not sure he really deserved.

Hank's tough upbringing made him suspicious of all strangers, and although his lack of pretense was attractive, many found Hank difficult at times. Lum York, one of his bass players, says in an interview that "a lot of people didn't like Hank as a person. . . . You had to be around him to understand him."[58] Bob McNett found Hank "abrupt." On the Good Vibrations recording of Jim Owen's "Hank Williams: The Man, the Legend," McNett describes the way he was hired. Bob, who had never met Hank, was working for Patsy Montana when Hank came up to him backstage at the Louisiana Hayride and said only, "Can you take the introduction to 'Lovesick Blues'?" That was it. Bob played that same night and became a Drifting Cowboy. In Jay Caress's book, McNett describes the way he was fired when Hank disbanded the Hayride crew: "Hank came offstage quickly after a Louisiana Hayride appearance and said, 'I'm going to Texas tomorrow. If I call you, you have a job. If I don't, you don't'."[59] Ed Linn refers to Hank's "hard core of bitterness" and then quotes Jim Denny: "I never knew anybody I liked better than Hank, but I don't think I ever really got close to him. I don't know if anyone really could. He was so bitter. He thought everybody, in the final analysis, had some sort of angle on him. I suppose that's why everybody has misinterpreted him. Because despite it all he was very kind and generous and very determined to be the top man in his profession."[60] Sol Handwerger, publicity director of MGM Records, says that Hank "was a most friendly person—provided he believed in your sincerity; if he did not, he could be cold and blunt." Handwerger saw Hank through a publicity tour of New York and found him "cynical and suspicious of big cities."[61] Roger Williams sums it up well when he says that the paradox of Hank was that the "insecurity and depth of feeling that nurtured his creative genius also drove him to self-ruin."[62]

Hank's personality and his physical situation seemed to nurture his bad habits. He was taking painkillers for his back problem, and he overdid the medication. Moreover, his binge drinking meant that he was either not drinking at all or he was completely ruined. His binges grew closer and closer together until they began merging just before his death. He had a low tolerance for alcohol and got drunk so quickly that it was almost impossible to intervene. Even when he was being watched carefully, adoring fans or hangers-on had a bad way of getting vodka to Hank. The privilege of fame meant that he could get it even from the attendants at the sanitarium. He hid airline bottles in his boots. Supposedly, he once tried to bribe Hillous Butrum for drinks, promising Hillous a recording contract, swearing he could get it for him because he had gotten one for Audrey. That he almost never ate when he was drinking helped wreck his health. Sammy Pruett says, "I've seen him drunk to where he couldn't hold water on his stomach. He'd be foaming at the mouth like a goddamned mad dog."[63] Hank was about 6 foot 1 inch and probably never weighed much over 140 pounds; usually he weighed much less. His suits had to be specially altered; the band called him "Gimly-ass" or "Bones." Chet Flippo says Hank could change clothes in a shotgun barrel.[64]

Obviously, drink was not a problem that sprang up with fame. Hank had been at it a long time, practically since childhood. He was in the Prattville, Alabama hospital in 1945 and was confined to the Madison Sanitarium, "The Hut," as early as the fall of 1949. In the fall of 1950, he was drunk at the Hippodrome in Baltimore and introduced Don Helms four times. He was drunk at that Last Frontier performance in Las Vegas. Hank fell off the stage in Peterborough, Ontario. The crowd was angry, and the Mounties had to see Hank safely out of town. Chet Flippo discovered that Hank went into North Louisiana Sanitarium on 21 May 1951, taken there by ambulance and treated by Dr. G. H. Cassity with Demerol, vitamin B, and Vitadex. He was complaining of severe back pain; x-rays revealed the spina bifida occulta, and Dr. Cassity fitted him with a lumbosacral brace. He was discharged on 24 May.[65]

The various treatments, all of them brief, could not rescue Hank. He would still go on sprees: hole up at the Hermitage Hotel and shoot up the room a little or check into the Tulane Hotel and get drunk. Supposedly, he ran naked down the hall after a lady wrestler similarly out of her clothes. One report has it that he tried to shoot a maid in Chattanooga and that he shot the portraits off the wall in a Birmingham hotel. His worst hotel episode occurred in 1952, at the New York Savoy, where in a drunken fit he pushed Frank Walker down against a radiator; he left Walker unconscious and apparently never realized what happened. When in trouble, Hank often passed himself off as "Herman P. Willis" or as George Morgan, who he disliked because that singer's hit "Candy Kisses" competed with Hank's songs. Then, too, the police indulged him because of his fame.

Hank was becoming less and less dependable, and bookings were more difficult to come by. Then he aggravated his back problem in a fall he took trying to jump a gully while squirrel hunting with Jerry Rivers. Jerry had to carry him back to the car. Not long thereafter, on 13 December 1951, Hank was admitted to the Vanderbilt University Hospital for a spinal fusion. He came out on Christmas Eve, wearing a back brace and taking more of the painkillers that complicated his miserably rundown health. According to Rivers, Hank was never quite himself again: "Hank began to indicate periods of mental depression and personal conflict in addition to the discomfort and pain from his injury, from which he never fully recovered. After his operation and subsequent convalescence Hank never seemed to regain the close personal relationship with the band and his friends that he had once enjoyed, and all of us had shared."[66] The band was already playing with Ray Price during the time that was left open by Hank's cancellations and by his stay in the hospital.

Hank's surgery and his need to use a walking cane briefly did not soften Audrey. They fought on, and soon after his homecoming, Hank shot up the place on Franklin Road. As she recounts the moment, Lycrecia implies that the problem was not just the drink and the drugs or the frustration at having to cancel an important New Year's Eve appearance in Baltimore. Rather, or perhaps in addition, Hank was angry because Audrey was determined to perform in his place. No one could possibly read the mind of Hank Williams at this moment, but he might well have been shooting at his wife. Audrey, who had stashed the kids with neighbors, went on to the Baltimore show, where she made Hank's apology—to the effect that he was not drunk but recovering from surgery. She sang with the Drifting Cowboys and, shortly afterward, called Hank to say she would not be back.[67] He would be dead in a year to the day.

Hank vacated the Franklin Road house quickly, on 3 January 1952. Audrey filed for separate maintenance a week later. She cited cruel and inhumane treatment and asked for nearly everything Hank had, including their son, and half of everything he was going to get. Hank was just too broken down to fight; he felt that he had to accept the terms, and, of course, he went on another drinking binge.

Now completely on his own, Hank approached one of his worst performances. He was scheduled to appear on 29 and 30 January 1952 in Richmond, Virginia, a show promoted by B. C. Gates. The fans had been voting a "Hillbilly of the Month," and Gates was bringing in the winners. Hank was roaring drunk by matinee time on 29 January, and Ray Price had to stall the crowd by singing, apologizing for Hank, and then declaring a thirty-minute intermission. Hank finally came on to stumble through a couple of songs. He was so bad that many fans started demanding refunds. Ray Price sang again. Then Hank gave it another try; he started by explaining that he had had back surgery and offered to show the crowd his scars or to have a doctor come and verify his problem. The show was a disaster, and a second performance was still to come that night. Some food, coffee, and a long walk in the cold straightened him out enough to get him through the next performance, but he was no hit. Howard Watts was so disgusted that he pulled out for Nashville.

The *Richmond Times-Dispatch* ran a scathing review the following day (30 January 1952). Edith Lindeman, the author of the review, noted that Hank's spine "most certainly was not holding him erect. He sang 'Cold, Cold, Heart,' but did not get some of the words in the right places. Then he sang 'Lonesome Blues,' with a good deal of off-key yodeling." The balance of the review was not much kinder.

Edith Lindeman's review, however, produced a good effect. Jim Denny had sent Charlie Sanders to Richmond to keep Hank straight for the shows. Sanders did not earn his keep on the first night, but the review produced new zeal. He got rid of Hank's booze and got the singer some medical attention, which probably involved some Demerol, allowing Hank to sleep off much of the problem of the moment. Hank was on his feet for the 30 January show. After Ray Price's introduction, he came on to do "Mind Your Own Business," dedicated to Edith Lindeman. The crowd loved it; and for one of the last times, Hank was really in charge of his audience.

Nashville, however, held little for him. He had to face up to the divorce, which became final on 29 May 1952, just a few days from the anniversary of his first divorce. Audrey got what she wanted, including half of all royalties still to come. She avoided scrupulously the remarriage that would have meant forfeiture of her claims on Hank. He got his cars, the farm at Franklin with its considerable mortgage, the clothing store, visitation rights, and a bill for $4,000 from Audrey's lawyer, Carmack Cochran. Hank signed over power of attorney to Sam Hunt and then disappeared briefly. He told Ray Price later that he had been hospitalized in Lexington, Kentucky, the indication being that he was in the federal narcotics hospital there.

The scene was pretty wild out on Natchez Trace in Nashville, where Hank was living with Ray Price. Hank was often drunk and/or hauling women in and out of the place. His guns, cigarettes, whiskey, and drugs made him a constant menace to himself and everyone else. Price finally had to move out on him.

Hank did a bad tour of California, where he stumbled through shows in Bakersfield, San Diego, Long Beach, and Oakland. Minnie Pearl was just coming off stage in San Diego when she saw Hank enter the auditorium:

I got off just in time to see this pathetic, emaciated, haunted-looking, tragic figure of a man being assisted through the stage door—not too gently—by a male nurse. The male nurse had undoubtedly had enough problems with Hank to warrant being impatient with him, but it upset me to see my friend handled that way....I ran to him and hugged him. He threw his arms around me and clung to me, crying. I tried to comfort him, to tell him that everything was going to be all right, just as you would try to comfort a child crying in the dark. No one will ever know what tortured dreams he had. Perhaps all of life was a bad dream to Hank. By this time he was killing himself with drugs and alcohol, and his mind had undoubtedly been affected.[68]

Minnie spent much of that evening trying to sober Hank up.

Trips to the sanitarium were almost routine by this time. Nothing seemed to make any difference: Hank was on his last legs. Yet, in the midst of this spiral down, he managed to record two big songs: a rollicking "Jambalaya" (MGM-11283) in June 1952 and, in July, the poignant "You Win Again" (MGM-11318). But he was struggling to make his Opry performances. Finally, after he missed a Friday night WSM show, The Grand Ole Opry fired Hank Williams. Jim Denny, who had done as much as anyone to keep Hank going, phoned the word on 11 August. Hank had been on the Opry a little over three years.

Apparently, Hank was not startled when Denny called. He was not expecting much, and he began to get ready to head back to Montgomery. From there he would go on to Shreveport, where he would return to the Louisiana Hayride, for $250 a week. Johnny Wright, husband of Kitty Wells and partner of Jack Anglin, drove Hank out of Nashville; he stopped only long enough for Hank to get his check and a bottle.

The next several weeks were really crowded. By 15 August, Hank was recovering in a fishing camp on Lake Martin, northeast of Montgomery and near the Creek Indian town of Kowaliga. The name, of course, inspired one of his most famous songs, "Kaw-Liga." Two days later he was in trouble in a small town nearby. Police Chief Winfred Patterson says that he arrested Hank in the Alexander City Hotel on 17 August 1952. According to Patterson, in an *Alabama Journal* interview of 20 February 1971, Hank "more or less was having DTs (delirium tremens). He was running up and down the hall, yelling that somebody was whipping old ladies and he was going to stop them."

The episode must have slowed Hank a bit, for he next turned up at his mother's in Montgomery. She put him in St. Jude's Hospital, where he continued a relationship with Father Harold Purcell, whom he had met during an earlier stay in the hospital, probably in 1950. Father Purcell worked with spastic children there. Lillie had practically eliminated Hank's visitors; and Purcell, who died in the fall of 1952, came to be much consolation to Hank. Purcell and St. Jude's must have helped Hank a little, for on 20 September he was back on the Hayride and on 23 September he was at the Castle Studios in Nashville for his last recordings, a really stunning session. Hank cut four sides: "I Could Never Be Ashamed of You," "Your Cheatin' Heart," "Kaw-Liga," and "Take These Chains from My Heart." His "I Could Never Be Ashamed" would back the previously recorded and seemingly prophetic "I'll Never Get out of This World Alive," which he had written with Fred Rose (MGM-11366). "Take These Chains," a Heath-Rose song, would back Hank's "Ramblin' Man" (MGM-11479). "Kaw-Liga," which he had written with Fred, and "Your Cheatin' Heart," which was altogether Hank's, came out on the same disc (MGM-11416). These two cuts—both about lost love, the first one wry and the second deeply sad—were just about perfect in catching the life and music of Hank Williams. That he could muster such performances in such a dark moment tells all we need to know about the mix of adversity and creativity, all we need to know about hard times and good music.

Only a few days later, Hank was back at Lillie's. Allen Rankin, the *Montgomery Advertiser* columnist who followed Hank so closely, reported on 28 September 1952 that Hank's two Cadillacs were parked at 318 North McDonough, that neither of them was being driven. Rankin went on rather dramatically, "Inside, Hank, too, lay still for a while. He had slipped on the pavement, hit his head and developed blood poison." A little over a week later, on 8 October, Hank wired Fred Rose: "Fred please send my checks to me in care of my mother Mrs Williams 318 North McDonough Montgomery Ala."[69] One wonders how much of Lillie's hand was in that message.

Things were as tough as usual at the boardinghouse, and additional problems were turning up fast. Lillie had taken in a woman, identified as "Bobbie Jett" in a *Montgomery Advertiser* story of 31 January 1968, and Bobbie Webb Jett was carrying the baby of Hank Williams. Hank had met

Bobbie in Nashville early in 1952. She had been born there in 1922 and had been left by her mother to grow up with relatives. As a young woman, she had gone off to California, where she married (or at least had a child by) a man named Tanquay. When she left California to return to Nashville and her relatives, she was traveling with a two- or three-year-old daughter, Jo Jett Tanquay.

Back in Nashville, Bobbie took a job with the Selective Service and conducted an active night life with the music folk. She met Hank and, in the spring of 1952, conceived his child. Apparently, she was traveling with him on the trip to Lake Martin, and clearly she and Jo were with him when he came down to Lillie's. The story, well told by Jett Williams (the daughter) in *Ain't Nothin' as Sweet as My Baby*, was that Hank and Bobbie were fairly casual in their relationship but that Hank took the pending paternity very seriously and thus took Bobbie to his mother's boardinghouse in Montgomery for the confinement. The deal, however, was going to get even stickier because Hank had still another woman to bring home to his mother's. He was head-over-heels after a new girlfriend, Billie Jean Jones Eshliman. Despite the presence of the pregnant Bobbie, he wanted to introduce Billie Jean to Lillie.

Billie Jean was a strikingly beautiful and naive telephone operator, the daughter of a Bossier City policeman. Jerry Rivers told me that "she couldn't ring a doorbell."[70] She had quit school in the twelfth grade and had married an airman, Harrison Eshliman, on 4 June 1949. Their child, Jerry Lynn, was born on 11 March the following year; but the marriage was fading fast, and Billie Jean had shown up in Nashville with Faron Young, who had been performing with the Louisiana Hayride. Hank met Billie Jean backstage at the Opry and, as the frequently told story goes, immediately pledged to marry her. The tale continues that Hank and Faron double-dated that night and, before the evening was out, switched girlfriends. Faron claims that Hank got about "half stoned" that evening, called him into a bedroom of the Natchez Trace house, pointed a pistol at him, and said: "I don't want no hard feelings out of you, but I'm in love with Billie Jean."[71] Hank took

Billie Jean—maybe thoughts of her brought him solace as he left Nashville. She was no happy lover, though, when she got to Lillie's to find the pregnant ex-girlfriend, Bobbie Jett. Billie Jean left for Shreveport, quickly and without her new boyfriend.

Hank got busy patching up the romance. The main item of business was taking care of things with Bobbie, which he did with a legal contract on 15 October 1952. In it Hank agreed to pay Bobbie's room and board from 15 October to 15 January 1953, and he gave his mother—who never seemed to miss a commercial opportunity, even when it came to a grandchild—$172 to cover the expense. Hank also agreed to give Bobbie $100 a month until the birth for the same period, to give her $200 if the child died, and to buy Bobbie a one-way ticket to any place she chose in California, the ticket to be used within seventy-five days of the birth. He agreed that the child was to have, and to use in all legal documents, its mother's name. He stipulated that Lillie was to have custody of the child for its first two years, while he paid all expenses and provided a nurse. Both Hank and Bobbie were to have generous visitation rights. When the child reached the age of three, Hank was to have custody, and when it reached the age of five, the parents were to have joint custody (summers and holidays with its mother, the rest of the year with Hank). Finally, because "paternity is in doubt," Bobbie Jett was to give up any future claims against Hank Williams.

The contract, prepared by Montgomery attorney Robert B. Stewart, worked, and Hank took his last bride. On 18 October 1952, just three days after he had filed his agreement with Bobbie Jett, Hank married Billie Jean in Minden, Louisiana before Justice of the Peace P. E. Burton. The marriage documents indicate that Billie Jean Jones Eshliman was white and twenty, Hiram Hank Williams white and thirty.[72] Hank had missed his age by a year: he was almost exactly twenty-nine and would never see the thirty he imagined.

The story of their wedding night is the traditional one of complications. The couple's car supposedly ran out of gas and they had to hitch a ride home. Hank reportedly invited their benefactor to come along for the

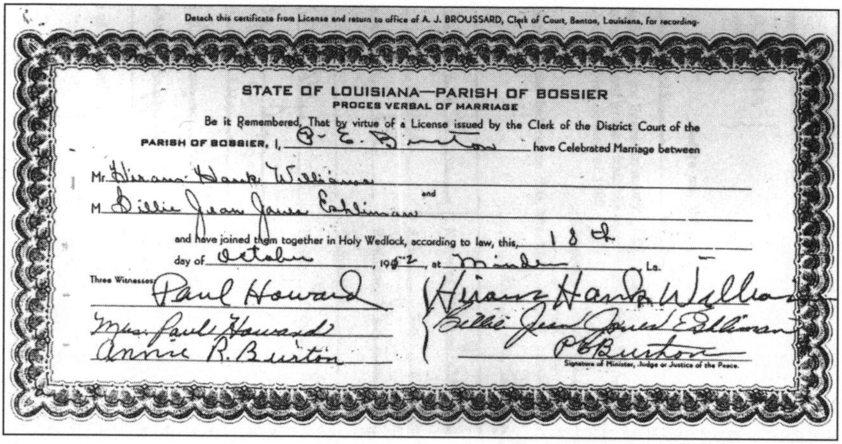

Detach this certificate from License and return to office of A. J. BROUSSARD, Clerk of Court, Benton, Louisiana, for recording.

STATE OF LOUISIANA—PARISH OF BOSSIER

PROCES VERBAL OF MARRIAGE

Be it Remembered, That by virtue of a License issued by the Clerk of the District Court of the PARISH OF BOSSIER, I, P. E. Burton have Celebrated Marriage between

Mr. Hiram Hank Williams

and

M. Billie Jean Jones Eshliman

and have joined them together in Holy Wedlock, according to law, this, 18th day of October, 1952, at Minden La.

Three Witnesses: Paul Howard

Mrs. Paul Howard

Annie R. Burton

Hiram Hank Williams

Billie Jean Jones Eshliman

P E Burton

Signature of Minister, Judge or Justice of the Peace.

Figure 14. Hank and Billie Jean's wedding certificate, dated 18 October 1952.

celebration; the gentleman declined discreetly. However, the events of that night were all preliminary. Hank and Billie Jean were going to marry again the next day, twice as a matter of fact, at a three o'clock matinee and at a seven o'clock evening performance at the New Orleans Civic Auditorium. Oscar Davis, best known for bringing Elvis and Colonel Parker together, knew how to turn a buck, and he was not going to miss this opportunity. Davis promoted the show, sold out the 14,000 seats twice at prices ranging from 75¢ to $1.50, and solicited wedding gifts for the newlyweds from local merchants. One minister refused to perform the ceremony, either because the marriage had been pronounced once already or because Hank had gotten into the champagne too soon. But L. R. Shelton, pastor of the First Baptist Church of Algiers, Louisiana was less scrupulous. He married the couple before the admiring fans, who got to hear a Hank Williams concert as well as see the wedding. Hank, though, was in bad shape when it was all over. He had to cancel the planned honeymoon to Cuba because he simply could not travel, and he and Billie Jean honeymooned at the Jung Hotel in New Orleans.

Figure 15. Hank and Billie Jean, the groom and bride. Photograph courtesy of Bruce Gidoll.

The new husband worked the Louisiana Hayride and toured the area for concerts. His bride traveled with him some. In a 1971 interview with Wesley Pruden, Billie Jean noted her naivete:

> I was awful young and didn't know much. I hadn't ever been anywhere, or done anything. When I married Hank, I hadn't ever stayed in a hotel. I didn't even have a suitcase. We stayed in the good hotels, but I still carried my shoes in one hand and all my things in a big Kotex box. I didn't even know enough to get another kind of box; it didn't embarrass me, and I guess Hank thought I was kind of cute. He never said anything. He carried my iron. I didn't even know they made travel irons, and I'd never heard of valets in hotels.[73]

She was naive about more than Kotex boxes: Billie Jean's divorce from Harrison Eshliman, filed on 25 September 1952, was not final until 28 October 1952.[74] Hank had married Audrey fifty days before the end of the sixty-day reconciliation period prescribed in her divorce decree; he married Billie Jean ten days before she was legally divorced from her first husband. The second rush to marry would cause the bride a lot of grief in her claims on Hank's estate.

Billie Jean worked hard at straightening Hank out. She tried to see that he ate and that he did not drink. But Hank was so deeply into booze and pills that he could not be stopped, not even by this beautiful young woman. Billie Jean sent him to the North Louisiana Sanitarium on 31 October, again on 27 November, and still again on 11 December.[75] The trips did not help much, and Hank's career was tearing downhill. He was so undependable that local promoters would not handle him. He had to make all of his own arrangements. This star who had been getting $1,500 for a show had to take whatever he could hustle, and he botched a good many of those shows. Hank was nearly mobbed in Lafayette, Louisiana for refusing to sing "Lovesick Blues," and Lillie had pulled him off stage in Biloxi, Mississippi to be flown home to her care in Montgomery.

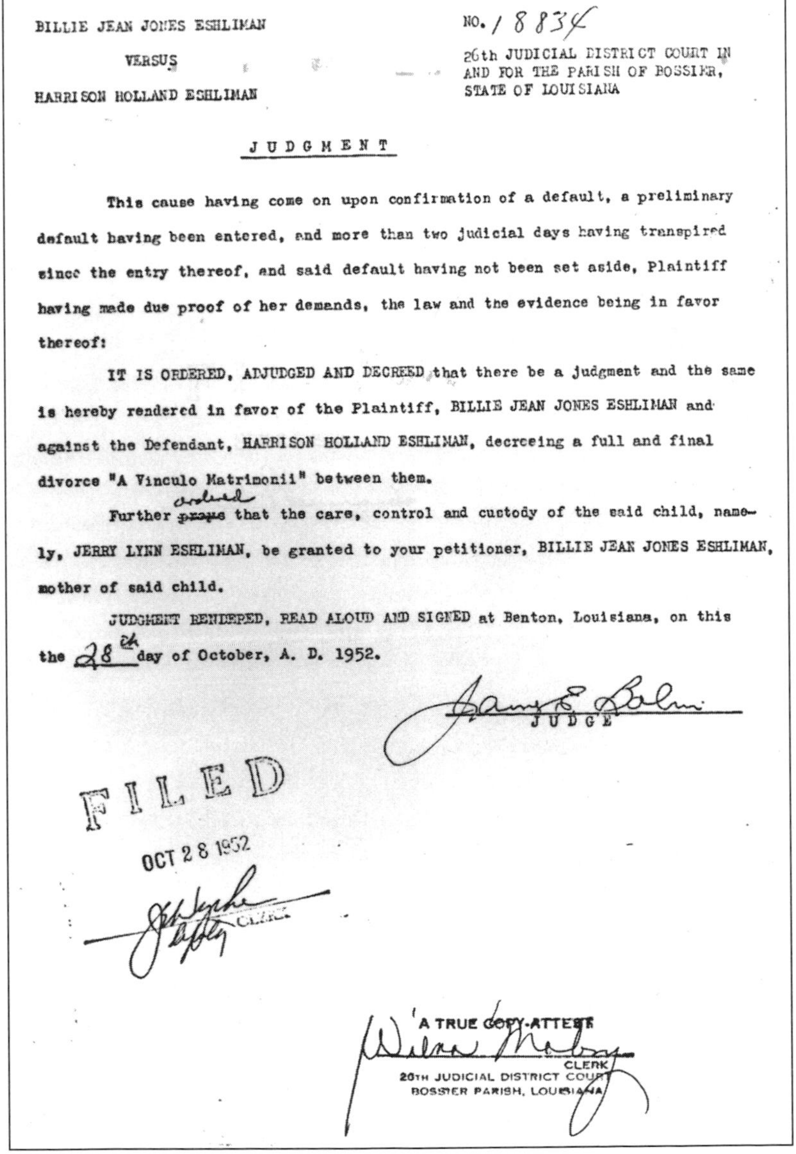

BILLIE JEAN JONES ESHLIMAN

VERSUS

HARRISON HOLLAND ESHLIMAN

NO. 18834

26th JUDICIAL DISTRICT COURT IN
AND FOR THE PARISH OF BOSSIER,
STATE OF LOUISIANA

JUDGMENT

This cause having come on upon confirmation of a default, a preliminary default having been entered, and more than two judicial days having transpired since the entry thereof, and said default having not been set aside, Plaintiff having made due proof of her demands, the law and the evidence being in favor thereof:

IT IS ORDERED, ADJUDGED AND DECREED that there be a judgment and the same is hereby rendered in favor of the Plaintiff, BILLIE JEAN JONES ESHLIMAN and against the Defendant, HARRISON HOLLAND ESHLIMAN, decreeing a full and final divorce "A Vinculo Matrimonii" between them.

Further ordered that the care, control and custody of the said child, namely, JERRY LYNN ESHLIMAN, be granted to your petitioner, BILLIE JEAN JONES ESHLIMAN, mother of said child.

JUDGMENT RENDERED, READ ALOUD AND SIGNED at Benton, Louisiana, on this the 28th day of October, A. D. 1952.

_____
JUDGE

FILED

OCT 28 1952

_____
CLERK

'A TRUE COPY-ATTEST

_____
CLERK
26TH JUDICIAL DISTRICT COURT
BOSSIER PARISH, LOUISIANA

Figure 16. The divorce decree of Billie Jean and Harrison Eshliman, issued on 28 October 1952. Billie Jean had married Hank ten days earlier.

As if his problems were not already enough, Hank got involved with a fake doctor, Horace Raphol "Toby" Marshall, whom he had met in Oklahoma City. Born in Michigan in 1901, Marshall had moved west to do time in San Quentin for forgery and armed robbery. He had gone into Oklahoma State Penitentiary on 15 October 1950 on a three-year sentence for forgery, but was paroled on 9 October 1951.[76] Marshall was a high school dropout who claimed a B.S. degree, an M.A., and a "D.S.C." He had bought the latter for $35 from the Chicago School of Applied Science. According to Jay Caress, Marshall had the diploma printed "D.S.C." to stand for "Doctor of Science and Psychology."[77] Marshall was a reformed alcoholic who claimed that he could help Hank. Actually, he was little more than a drug contact who, with a series of fraudulent prescriptions, some of them written in the name of Dr. C. W. Lemon, kept Hank in amphetamines, Seconal, chloral hydrate, and morphine. His last prescription for Hank, written when the singer was in Oklahoma in December 1952, was for twenty-four grains of chloral hydrate, a sedative that depresses the central nervous system. Hank filled and then refilled the prescription in Montgomery. Within less than a month, Hank Williams would be dead and his family would receive a bill for $736.39 from Dr. Marshall.

The frantic activity of the last few months slowed somewhat just before Christmas. Hank and Billie Jean went to Georgiana to see Hank's cousin, Taft Skipper, and his wife Erleen. They arrived late on 21 December, a Sunday, and went to church with the Skippers. Hank turned down requests to sing that night, but the next morning he did a few songs at Taft's store; one of them was "The Log Train," a fine number that Hank had written for his father and one that was not issued until 1982. Hank and Billie Jean then went on to Lillie's in Montgomery. On Christmas Day, they drove over to McWilliams to see Lon, who had gone to Selma for the holiday. Hank wanted to sing "The Log Train" to his father, but he had to be content to leave some gifts and return to Lillie's. On 27 December, Taft and his niece, Mary Skipper, drove up to Montgomery and went with Hank and Billie Jean to the Blue-Gray football game. Taft and Mary had good seats down close to the field; but Hank and Billie Jean were in the upper stands, and the cold sent them home at halftime.

The next night, Hank performed for the Montgomery chapter of the American Federation of Musicians. The group was raising money for Charlie Davis, a radio announcer and drummer who was recovering from polio. In his column in the *Montgomery Advertiser* the next day, Allen Rankin described Hank as "a thin, tired-looking ex-country boy with a guitar. He got up and sang (or howled) a number of his tunes that started out to be hillbilly but ended up as 'pop' numbers played and sung by every band in the land."[78] Like a good many writers then and now, Rankin did not seem sure of just how seriously he should take Hank Williams. But his tone would change in a few days, and very shortly he would be ghostwriting Lillie's book on Hank.

Hank was well received by the American Federation of Musicians group that night, and he was almost certainly thinking of a return to The Grand Ole Opry. Some believe that those hopes of Nashville included reconciliation with Audrey, but evidence of that is hard to find. Further hope of career revival had come when Hank accepted an offer to play a New Year's Day show in Canton, Ohio. A. V. Bamford of Nashville had booked it for him. It would be Hank's first date out of the South since he left the Opry, and it might have been a step back to the stage of Ryman Auditorium. Hank had good feelings about Canton; he had played well there on 27 April 1951, while at the height of his success. The Drifting Cowboys were already booked into Cleveland with Ray Price, but Don Helms agreed to come to Canton and to bring with him guitarist Autry Inman.

A rare snowstorm hit Montgomery on 30 December, and that meant no flying for Hank. Still eager to get to the show, he hired Charles Harold Carr, an eighteen-year-old Auburn freshman who sometimes worked for his father at the Lee Street Taxi Company, to drive the baby-blue Cadillac convertible for the twenty hours it would take to get to Canton. Hank was in rough shape. He had been in a fight sometime during the visit home. His habit was to return to old haunts while in Montgomery, and he was usually eager to display his success. The bragging had gotten him into more than one brawl. Hank left Montgomery this time with his left arm, either sprained or broken, in a bandage. How he managed his good-byes to his mother, the very pregnant Bobbie Jett, and his wife must have been interesting. Colin Escott cites the familiar story that, as he left for this last journey, Hank gave $50 to Marie Harvell, a relative of Lillie's who lived at the boarding-house. The money was to pay for Bobbie's cab fare to and from St. Mar-garet's Hospital.[79] For many reasons, Hank must have been glad to be hit-ting the road again.

He and Carr took Highway 31 to Birmingham, where they spent the first night at the Redmont Hotel. Then it was up Highway 11 to Chattanooga and on into Knoxville. Hank, quick to get on with his old habits, was drink-ing beer and taking chloral hydrate while Carr drove. In Knoxville, they caught a 3:30 P.M. flight for Ohio, but bad weather forced the plane back to Knoxville. The two travelers then headed for the Andrew Johnson Hotel, where Carr checked them in at 7:08 P.M. The assistant hotel manager, Dan McCrary, talked to a nervous Charles Carr but did not see Hank, who was carried up to a room by porters.

Carr ordered two steaks, but Hank was unable to eat. Dr. P. H. Card-well arrived and noted that Hank was extremely drunk and that he was carrying several capsules. Cardwell gave Hank two vitamin B12 shots, each of which contained one-quarter grain of morphine. The B12 was probably for the vitamin deficiency standard in alcoholics. The morphine could have been for Hank's back pain, but it is also a recognized treatment for pul-monary edema, excess fluid in the lungs. Hank's fight might have caused the edema, but the condition is symptomatic of drug overdose as well. Hank could have been subject to the problem on both counts. Why Carr and Cardwell did not get Hank to a hospital remains a mystery. Perhaps they were frightened or perhaps they were disgusted with their obviously inebriated patient. Besides, Carr still seemed intent on getting Hank to Canton in time to rest before the show; he was well aware that Hank's contract carried a $1,000 default penalty. He got the porters to help dress

Hank and then carry the singer back out to the Cadillac. Hank showed no sign of life except for a slight cough when he was picked up. Carr checked them out of the Andrew Johnson at 10:45 P.M.

At 11:45 P.M. Carr was stopped for reckless driving near Blaine, Tennessee. He had been trying to pass a car and had nearly run head on into Patrol Corporal Swann H. Kitts. When the patrolman questioned Carr about the lifeless-looking man on the back seat, Carr explained that Hank had been drinking and had taken a sedative. Kitts accepted the story and led the travelers into Rutledge, Tennessee, where Carr paid his $25 fine to Magistrate Olin H. Marshall. Carr then drove on toward Canton, picking up relief driver Donald Surface in Bristol, Tennessee. Just about dawn on New Year's Day, in Oak Hill, West Virginia, Carr finally decided to check on his famous passenger. He pulled into Glen Burdette's Pure Oil station and reached back to find Hank cold. Patrolman Howard Jamey came to the scene and led Carr to the Oak Hill Hospital where, at 7:00 A.M., Dr. Diego Nunnari, an intern, declared Hank dead. The body was taken to the Tyree Funeral Home and embalmed.

Meanwhile, the show went on in Canton. The master of ceremonies, Cliff Rodgers, a local disc jockey, arranged a single spotlight on an empty stage. Rodgers stepped into the light and made the startling announcement that the twenty-nine-year-old singer was dead. The audience, aware of Hank's habit of missing shows, laughed at what they took to be the ultimate in bad excuses. But Rogers assured them of the truth and then stepped out of the spot. The cast, gathered behind the curtain, sang "I Saw the Light," with more than a few of the 4,000 fans joining in. The regular show then went on with performances by Hawkshaw Hawkins, Homer and Jethro, and June Webb.

The details of the events in and around Knoxville are fortuitously available to us for one reason: When Captain John Davis of the Tennessee Highway Patrol heard of Hank's death and of the involvement of one of his patrolmen, he ordered Kitts to investigate Hank's passage through Knoxville. Kitts made a thorough investigation and filed a handwritten report that

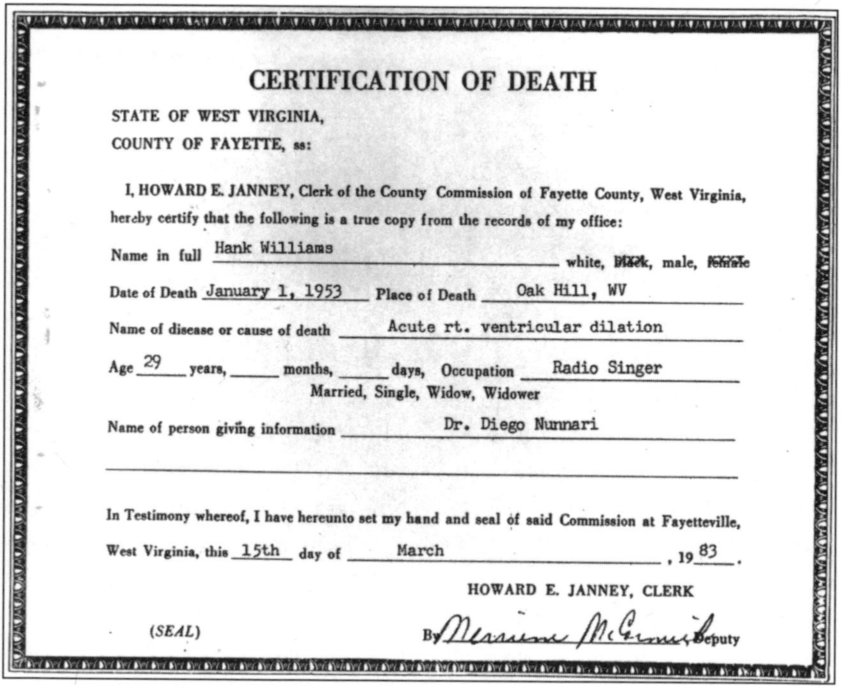

CERTIFICATION OF DEATH

STATE OF WEST VIRGINIA,
COUNTY OF FAYETTE, ss:

I, HOWARD E. JANNEY, Clerk of the County Commission of Fayette County, West Virginia, hereby certify that the following is a true copy from the records of my office:

Name in full Hank Williams white, ~~black~~, male, ~~female~~

Date of Death January 1, 1953 Place of Death Oak Hill, WV

Name of disease or cause of death Acute rt. ventricular dilation

Age 29 years, ____ months, ____ days, Occupation Radio Singer
Married, Single, Widow, Widower

Name of person giving information Dr. Diego Nunnari

In Testimony whereof, I have hereunto set my hand and seal of said Commission at Fayetteville, West Virginia, this 15th day of March, 1983.

HOWARD E. JANNEY, CLERK

(SEAL) By Mervine McCormick Deputy

Figure 17. Hank's death certificate.

includes the details I have cited. The *Knoxville Journal* made the report public in a story on 15 December 1982.

Kitts made these interesting comments as he concluded:

> After investigating this matter, I think that Williams was dead when he was dressed and carried out of the hotel. Since he was drunk and was given the injections and could have taken some capsules earlier, with all this he couldn't have lasted over an hour and a half or two hours. A man drunk or doped will make some movement if you move them. A dead man will make a coughing sound if they are lifted around. Taking all this into consideration, he must have died in Knoxville at the hotel.[80]

Kitts's diagnosis includes no science, but the officer's speculation allows the terrifying possibility that Charles Carr, who checked out of a hotel less than three hours after he had checked in, frantically drove a dead Hank Williams out of Knoxville, practically ran a patrolman off the highway, paid a quick fine, and then drove on until breaking day finally convinced him that he had to stop and face the situation. The other possibility has life slowly leaving the comatose Hank Williams somewhere between Knoxville and Oak Hill as one year faded into another.

Lillie arrived in Oak Hill and was joined quickly by Toby Marshall, a conjunction that leads many of us to believe that the two had worked together to keep Hank going, a project that only supplied the singer with his last drugs. The grief-stricken mother demanded Hank's jewelry and an autopsy. Dr. Ivan M. Malinin's autopsy reveled alcoholic cardiomyopathy, heart disease traceable directly to excessive drinking. The death certificate, filed in the county seat, Fayetteville, West Virginia, cited the cause of death as "acute ventricular dilation." A coroner's jury viewed the body and, on 10 January, confirmed the verdict. On 11 January, the *Montgomery Advertiser* quoted that group's report to Magistrate Virgil Lyons: "We the jury find on January 10 that Hank Williams died of a severe heart condition and hemorrhage. No evidence was found of foul play." The blood contained alcohol, but, according to Lyons, no indication of narcotics or other drugs. The hemorrhages were in the heart and in the neck; because they were not consistent with the heart failure, some suspect that they were the result of the Montgomery fight. Hank had lived so carelessly, though, that he could have died from any number of causes. The autopsy, performed on an embalmed body, was neither very sophisticated nor very thorough; it was so amateurish, in fact, that it found no sign of drugs. The very immediate cause of Hank Williams's death remains obscure, as shrouded as the moment of death.

Lillie sent the body home to Montgomery, to her place on North McDonough Street, and began planning the funeral for 4 January 1953. She wanted to have it at the Highland Baptist Church, but obviously the sanctuary was not large enough. The confusion was intense, with Audrey and Billie Jean both at the house; Bobbie Jett, who was just a couple of days away from delivery; not to mention Lillie and Lon. Audrey and Lillie teamed up to practically exclude Billie Jean. Lon, who Lillie had generously listed as "deceased" on the death certificate, would not even get to sit with the family at the funeral. Lycrecia was sent off to stay with Audrey's parents and would miss the funeral altogether.

Fortunately, A. V. Bamford, the promoter who had booked Hank into Canton, showed up to make the arrangements. The city donated the use of its auditorium, and Bamford scheduled a 2:30 P.M. funeral for 4 January. About 25,000 people showed up for what Roger Williams says "is regarded in Montgomery as the greatest emotional plunge the city has taken since the inauguration of Jefferson Davis as president of the confederacy."[81]

Some 3,000 of the mourners went inside the auditorium when the doors opened at 1:15 P.M. A good many of those had time to file by and gaze at Hank Williams, laid out in an open silver casket, holding a small white Bible that could not have been his. Those who could not get in listened over loudspeakers outside or picked up the service on one of the two radio stations that carried it. Ernest Tubb began by singing "Beyond the Sunset." A black quartet, the Southwind Singers, followed; they especially pleased the 200 or so blacks seated in the auditorium's balcony. Dr. Henry Lyon of the Highland Baptist Church read the Twenty-Third Psalm. He preached briefly, saying that Hank had gone to the last round-up, that Hank's funeral sermon had actually been preached already in his songs. Roy Acuff—with Red Foley, Carl Smith, Webb Pierce, and many others in the chorus—sang "I Saw the Light." Foley sang "Peace in the Valley," and the Statesmen Quartet finished with "Precious Memories."

Hank was buried in Montgomery's Oakwood Cemetery Annex, an unpretentious place within easy walking distance of the state capitol building. A good bit of urban blight borders the cemetery. The police department and the city jail are nearby; bail-bonding companies cluster in the area. His first grave crowded Hank in near the graves of a number of French flyers who had been killed in a training accident, but he was to get a better spot soon. On 17 January 1953, his body was moved a short distance to a soft knoll that allows a fairly scenic view. His monument was unveiled during a Hank Williams Memorial celebration on 20–21 September 1954. The affair, attended by an estimated 60,000 people, included dances played by Ray Price, Pee Wee King, and Jim Reeves. The celebration had a huge parade with many Opry stars, but featuring Lillie in Hank's car. The Alabama Air National Guard did some fancy flying overhead, and Roy Acuff starred in a memorial show. Jimmie Davis, former governor of Louisiana and a good country songwriter, placed a wreath on Hank's grave at the unveiling of the tomb.

The marble monument, designed by Willie Gayle of the Henley Memorial Company, is distinct without being overwhelming. An upright slab is inscribed "Hank Williams." Just below the name is the two-line refrain of "I Saw the Light." A cowboy hat rests at the foot of the slab near a number of marble squares inscribed with the names of some of Hank's songs. The Luke the Drifter square is in the center, as if Willie Gayle wanted us to remember Hank as moralist. On the back of the slab is a poem written by the divorced but would-be widow, Audrey:

> Thank you for all the love you gave me
> There could be no one stronger
> Thank you for the many beautiful songs
> They will live long and longer
> Thank you for being a wonderful father to Lycrecia
> She loved you more than you knew
> Thank you for our precious son
> And thank God he looks so much like you
> And now can I say:
> There are no words in the dictionary
> That can express my love for you
> Someday beyond the blue
> > Audrey Williams

Figure 18. Hank's grave in Montgomery's Oakwood Cemetery Annex. The grave beside his plot is Lillie's. The last of the three stones beyond Lillie's grave belongs to Audrey. In Jun 1983, Hank Jr. and Lycrecia reinterred their mother beside Hank. Photograph by E. Denny.

A separate slab over the grave itself is marked simply with the name and the dates; a guitar and a pair of cowboy boots are carved into it. The slab, with all of its corners chipped away by souvenir hunters, is flanked by two urns and by two marble benches. The urns were originally cowboy boots, but vandals destroyed them.

Memorials to Hank, of course, came quickly and were numerous. The Sunday, 11 January 1953 *Montgomery Advertiser–Alabama Journal* was devoted to him, and it overflowed with testimonials by the news staff and by fans who had written in. Generally they were professions of grief and affection; sometimes they expressed hopes of meeting Hank in another life. One was a spelling testimonial: "H is for the heart for music, A is for his

Figure 19. Family and friends at the Hank Williams Memorial Picnic in 1982. From left to right: Taft Skipper, Erleen Skipper, Walt McNeil, J. C. McNeil, Ola Schuffert, and Braxton Schuffert. Photograph by E. Denny.

Alabama, N is for the nation's number one singer, K is for the king of the blues, W is for the will to be a success, I is for the island in the sky where he rests," and so on. Frank Walker wrote Hank a letter, in care of Songwriter's Paradise, wishing the deceased a happy New Year. His sister Irene wrote him, too, and predicted their ultimate reunion. Freddie Hart and Eddie Dean wrote a poem in which Hank's guitar, deserted now, speaks of its loneliness.

On 10 March 1953, John M. Gallalee, president of the University of Alabama, announced the school's Hank Williams Music Scholarship. American Folk Publications had given the first $1,000. The *Alabama Journal* noted the scholarship on 13 March, and one of its staff writers suggested some qualifications for the award. Recipients, he said, should have barely finished high school, should have slept through classes (especially English), should not know one note from another, and should have a voice like an electric saw; applicants should be sorrowful and should have "a high-voltage compulsion for trouble and a revulsion for calm things and peace of mind." Finally, though, the recipient should be a "natural" and, "in his field, a genius." That mix of the facetious with the serious has been a part of the commentary on Hank Williams ever since.

In 1974, the Butler County Historical Association marked Hank's birthplace with a plaque that is unaffected in its simple statement that Hank was a "world famous composer and performer of country music." Unfortunately, quarrels among the various groups eager to be responsible for Hank's memory in Butler County resulted in the moving of the plaque from the birth site to a small Hank Williams park nearby. The best-known memorial, and the most appropriate one, was placed in the Country Music Hall of Fame in Nashville when Hank, Jimmie Rodgers, and Fred Rose became the first members in 1961. After the name and the dates, it reads: "Performing artist, songwriter... Hank Williams will live on in the memories of millions of Americans. The simple beautiful melodies and straight-forward plaintive stories in his lyrics of life as he knew it will never die. His songs appealed not only to the country music field, but brought him great acclaim in the pop music world as well."

THE AFTERMATH

Hank left no will, no life insurance. His estate was negligible, it seemed: He had a cashier's check on the First National Bank of Montgomery for $4,000 and about $9,000 worth of personal items. He had been making little money, and Audrey was getting half of that. But his name and his songs were going to be worth quite a bit. The *Billboard* people were compiling their 1952 charts just as Hank died. He had three songs well ranked: "Jambalaya" (3), "Half as Much" (11), and "Honky Tonk Blues" (28). Hank's music was to be even more popular in 1953, when the *Billboard* chart had "Kaw-Liga" (1), "Your Cheatin' Heart" (2), and "Take These Chains from My Heart" (9). Obviously, the estate was going to be worth a fight.

Lon Williams, whether for the sake of dignity or fear of Lillie, bowed out graciously. Billie Jean lost out fast. The *Alabama Journal* of 14 January 1953 reported that Louisiana Judge James Brolin, the judge who had been slow about signing the divorce decree for Billie Jean in 1952, ruled that her marriage to Hank was illegal. But that did not keep her from going on the road as "Mrs. Hank Williams." Audrey went on the road under the same name and was playing a "Kaw-Liga Day" celebration near Lake Martin on 19 March 1953, just a few months into her grief.

The two talentless women, battling to be widow, headed for court that spring. But Billie Jean, perhaps dismayed by Judge Brolin's decision, accepted a $30,000 settlement whereby she gave up all claims to the name and estate. Audrey, who was sending a weekly wreath to Hank's grave, had the widowhood to herself. In July 1953, a Davidson County (Tennessee) Chancery Court gave her half of Hank's estate; near the end of August, Lillie got the other half and became administratrix and legal guardian of Hank Jr. when the boy, now almost four, was in Alabama. Otherwise, the child and his goods were in Audrey's care.

Lillie, who divorced W. W. Stone in April 1954, did not last very long. She died in her sleep on 26 February 1955 and was buried to Hank's left, within inches of the border of his plot. She seemed to be anxious to beat Audrey to his side, anxious to prove the statement she had made in her book: "Hank's mother was always his first girl and he never forgot it."[82]

Hank's sister, Irene Williams Smith, then became administratrix and Alabama guardian of Hank Jr., although her term was badly scarred. Audrey and Hank Jr. sued Irene in September 1966 for return of some of Hank's personal items. Then another mess arose: Irene had sold the renewal rights for Hank's music to Acuff-Rose for $25,000 in March 1963. The original rights were not due to expire for ten years, and many suspected that the sale was premature and the price ridiculous. Audrey and Hank Jr., just out of court in the first case, revisited that issue and sued again in the fall of 1967. But Judge Richard Emmett upheld the original renewal contract in a decree of 30 January 1968. Then Irene was arrested while crossing the border at Laredo with what the *Birmingham Post-Herald*, on 2 August 1969, called "one of the largest amounts of pure cocaine ever to enter the U.S." She was sentenced to seven years in the federal jail in Alderson, West Virginia. Montgomery attorney Robert B. Stewart, who had drafted the contract between Hank and Bobbie Jett, took over the estate. In a long and rather sad letter of 12 February 1984, Irene, then living in Dallas, explained to me, "I have maintained a very low profile the past few years with the hope that my past would not reflect on Hank." But Hank, I think, would have understood.

The other jail sentence in the aftermath of Hank's death went to Toby Marshall, D.S.C. While prescribing for Hank, Marshall had also prescribed drugs for his wife, Fay, who lived in Albuquerque. When she died on 3 March 1953, Governor Johnston Murray sprang to action and revoked Marshall's parole. Marshall stayed in jail only until 1 May 1954. But he was not out long; in September 1956 he started a one-year sentence for unlawful possession of barbiturates. One persistent rumor has it that Marshall, behind bars, wrote his own memoir with the basic premise that Hank committed suicide. No one I know of has seen that manuscript. But no one would be surprised that Marshall, so unscrupulous and so deeply involved in the end of Hank Williams, would make such a claim.

Audrey went home to the place on Franklin Road and stayed busy being Hank's widow—adding to the house, touring with her various all-girl bands (one of them ironically called "The Cold, Cold Hearts"), doing her own share of drugs and alcohol, generating much gossip with her affairs, and trying to shape Hank Jr. into the image of his father. She taught him both Hank's voice and songs, and the heir played his first show at age eight. He made the Opry at eleven and *The Ed Sullivan Show* at fourteen. In one particularly sad gesture, in 1964, Audrey arranged for him to do a New Year's Day show—in Canton, Ohio. As soon as he reached the legal age of eighteen, Hank Jr. declared his full independence of his mother and went on to a remarkable career that he still enjoys. He and his second wife, Gwen Yeargin, are the parents of Shelton Hank Williams, who tours now as Hank Williams III.[83] Lycrecia, once married to Lamar Morris, a member of Hank Jr.'s band, lives in Charlotte, North Carolina, with her three children.

Billie Jean married Johnny Horton in 1954 and dropped out of the Hank Williams picture for many years. But she was widowed again, on 5 November 1960, when Horton was killed in an automobile accident. She would turn back to Williams matters in a suit over the MGM movie *Your Cheatin' Heart*, which had premiered at Montgomery's Paramount Theatre on 4 November 1964. Audrey was the movie's technical adviser and, it seems, allowed little footage to be wasted on the competition. The film deftly ignored Hank's marriage to Billie Jean, and the offended party sued MGM for $4.5 million in October 1969. She lost the case, but sued again in March 1972. Her new case was against MGM, CBS, and Storer Broadcasting. CBS and Storer became involved because of television broadcasts of the film. In a peculiar decision, the jury declared Billie Jean the legal widow, said she was libeled, but awarded no damages. Billie Jean, however, was persistent; she sued again on 4 May 1972 when she took the 9 March decision for her widowhood into court against MGM, claiming that the studio showed malice in failing to destroy the movie and in continuing to market the sound track, neither of which acknowledged her legal status as Hank's second wife. She lost that case, too. But her flair for litigation may explain the notable scarcity of screenings of the film today. We can thank her for that.

Billie Jean did win one case, though. She sold her prospective interest in Hank's music to Hill and Range Publishers, and she and that company sued for a share of Hank's royalties. On 22 October 1975, U.S. District Court Judge L. Clure Morton ruled in Nashville that Billie Jean Berlin (she had since married N. Kent Berlin) had been Hank Williams's common-law wife and that she should have a part of the copyright renewals. When she divorced Berlin, she went back to being Mrs. Johnny Horton. Over the years, she has had little good to say about her marriage to Hank Williams, but, as we say, she continues to cash the checks. I understand that she lives well, near Shreveport, with the satisfaction that she outlived the competition.

Audrey, close to bankruptcy and in deep trouble with the IRS, died less than two weeks after the decision for Billie Jean. On 4 November 1975 she was found dead at the Franklin Road home. Audrey's death was of natural causes, but obviously drink and pills had done to her much the same damage that they had done to her spouse. Just before her death, in fact, she practically had been an invalid. After a small funeral in Troy, Alabama, she was taken to Montgomery and Oakwood Cemetery, where the Chaplain of Bourbon Street, Bob Harrington, read "Hey, Good Lookin'" at her interment. The most famous witness at the burial was George C. Wallace.

Because space near Hank and Lillie's graves was so scarce, Audrey was originally buried in the next family plot, that of the Smiths who were the in-laws of Irene Williams. Their space included six graves, five of them occupied at the time, one of them by an infant, Irene's child by J. T. Smith. The last grave, the one farthest from Hank's, became Audrey's. She rested there, as close to Hank as she could get, until June 1983, when Hank Jr. and Lycrecia arranged burial for her beside Hank where she lies now, with a monument matching his.

Lon Williams continued life in McWilliams, Alabama, with Ola Till, who he had married in 1942, and their daughter, Leila, born in 1943. Lon, who so wisely removed himself from the fray over the estate, was nearly eighty when he died on 23 October 1970 in Wilcox Memorial Hospital in Camden, Alabama. He is buried in Hopewell Methodist Cemetery near McWilliams. Hank's half-sister, Leila, now Mrs. Leila Williams Griffin, lives in nearby Selma.

Winding along behind all of this is the story of Jett Williams, the daughter of Hank and Bobbie Jett, the child born on 6 January 1953, just two days after the funeral of her father. Her original name was Antha Belle, for her two grandmothers on her mother's side of the family. The girl lived with Lillie and Bill Stone and was cared for primarily by Marie Harvell, Lillie's niece, who lived at the boardinghouse. When Lillie divorced Bill in April 1954, she maintained custody of the child. She went on to complete the adoption on 23 December 1954 and changed the girl's name to Catherine Yvone Stone—Catherine from *Wuthering Heights* and Yvone a misspelled version of a character from Hank's great song "Jambalaya." Then, just two months later, on 26 February 1955, Lillie died.

Hank's sister, Irene Williams Smith, now in charge of the estate, made it clear that she was not interested in Cathy and, with Bill Stone's permission, turned her over to the state welfare system. For a year, the child lived in a licensed home, in Pine Level, Alabama, managed by Mr. and Mrs. Henry Cook. Then, in February 1956, she met and moved in with Wayne and Louise Deupree in Mobile. The Deuprees completed the adoption in April 1959 and renamed the child Cathy Louise Deupree. Reference to Cathy turned up from time to time in the various litigations over the estate, particularly in the 1967 case between Irene and Audrey and Hank Jr. Her guardian ad litem, Drayton Hamilton, petitioned the court for the 1952 contract between Hank and Bobbie Jett. But after a hearing in August 1967, Judge Richard Emmet ordered the contract and the notes on the hearing sealed. In December of that year, Judge Emmet ruled that Hank Jr. was the sole heir to the estate; Billie Jean would have to get her share later. The Deuprees, eager to have their child and to let the matter rest, did not allow an appeal.

Bobbie Jett, Cathy's mother, did not rock the boat either. She had gone on to Nashville just after the birth and had signed there the "consent of parents to adoption" form in June 1953. Then she headed on to California, where she married John Tippins and had six more children before she died on 17 April 1974. She never made contact with her daughter in Alabama.

Just after turning twenty-one, Cathy learned that she might be the lost daughter of Hank Williams. Louise Deupree broke the news, but only because she understood that Cathy would soon receive a check for about $2,000 from the estate of Lillie Stone. Lillie had not included Cathy in her will, but apparently someone in the family, perhaps Irene, prescribed the payment as a gesture toward the stated intentions of Hank Williams. The check and the news, of course, stimulated Cathy, about to graduate from the University of Alabama and to marry Michael Mayer, to begin a serious search for her parents.

Cathy found her way back to the Cooks, her foster parents, then to Marie Harvell, and then to Bobbie's uncle, Willard Jett. By 1981, she had found and met her half-siblings in California. In the process, she discovered the 15 October 1952 contract between Hank and Bobbie, and she found that her identity had been suppressed in the 1967 court case. Her adoptive father, Wayne Deupree, was sympathetic about the search, but his fragile and alcoholic wife, Louise, was offended that Cathy was not content with just her adoptive parents. Wayne died in 1983; when Louise died a wealthy woman in 1987, she had completely disinherited Cathy.

Cathy's luck was not all dark, though. During a separation from her first husband, Cathy met Keith Adkinson, "a Washington attorney with a pick-up truck," as she puts it in her memoir. Adkinson led the many tangled legal battles that finally peaked in July 1989, when Alabama's supreme court ruled that Cathy was the legal daughter of Hank Williams and that she was entitled to be redressed by her father's estate. Hank Jr. appealed, but in 1993, Cathy finally made her point and won a share of the publishing and royalty wealth left by her father. She now splits the money with Hank Jr. and Billie Jean Horton.

By now, Cathy had divorced Mayer and married Keith Adkinson. This man turned out to be more than a lawyer and husband; he encouraged and promoted his bride in a singing career, which she pursues today, with a reconstituted Drifting Cowboys Band, under her most recent name, Jett Williams. An *Atlanta Journal-Constitution* story of 20 September 1998 reported that Jett and Hank III, a young man totally alienated from his father, first met when they were billed together at an outdoor concert. The two made it clear that no love was lost between them, and Hank III "laid down the challenge that he was going to 'blow her off the stage'." There the legacy of Hank Williams, with its spectacular music and its family tangles, stands today.

2

The Song: An Evaluation

Hank Williams, you wrote my life.

Hank Williams was in no shape to write any music the night he died, but this has not interfered with the persistent story that he clutched a last song in his dead hands when he and Charles Carr reached Oak Hill Hospital. The crumpled number went like this: "We met, we lived and dear we loved, then came that fatal day, the love that felt so dear fades away. Tonight love hathe one alone and lonesome, all that I could sing I you you [sic] still and always will, but that's the poison we have to pay."[1]

We may want to read the song as Hank's last testimony to his love for Audrey and thus get into that debate about whether he was headed back to her. But a more important and more certain element shows here: We cherish the idea that the great songwriter always worked spontaneously, pulling fine music from tortured experience, even at the moment of death. Hank Williams composing as he died is one of the more romantic images in the history of American arts. Although the scene has no historical basis, it is deeply imbedded in the mind of country music.

This image represents the authenticity that is the basis of genuine, or what many call "hard," country music. At its best, the genre is absolutely straightforward and unpretentious. Ideally, the performer sings about his own life in his own songs. He allows none of pop music's fantasy and does not separate himself from his fans with the antics familiar to rock. In short, hard country is democratic. Its performers seem to be speaking to their equals of real and often shared experience—thus, the importance of knowing that Jimmie Rodgers worked for the railroads he sang about, that his song "T. B. Blues" was about his own disease. And when Johnny Cash decided to sing about jail at Folsom Prison, he promoted the false idea that he had done a little time himself.

This demand for the connection of life and art may explain why country performers have to make so many personal appearances, why someone like Ernest Tubb had to show up at 200 different places each year, even at the height of his success. I think it also explains why country music generates so little criticism and so much biography and autobiography. To see the singers and comprehend their lives is to understand their music. The faces of Tubb, George Jones, Kitty Wells, Merle Haggard, and Willie Nelson are worth more than any number of producers and agents, the life stories of those stars worth more than most explorations of the folk origins of country music. Hank Williams is classic in this sense. Deciding whether his fans are more interested in his life or his work is practically impossible, and I am not sure that anyone knows whether his nickname, "Lovesick," came from life or art. The two items probably balance each other better in Hank than in any other singer, and they bring special satisfaction to hard country fans, who demand history, or at least myth, with their music.

The clearest and most interesting illustration of my point involves Hank's songwriting. He was untutored, a composer who could not write a note and could therefore preserve tunes only in his head or on demonstration records. He himself joked that he knew only two melodies, a fast one and a slow one. Like many great American naturals, Hank had learned much of his slight knowledge of music from a black man, the character stereotypically so sensitive to his own emotions. Like Jerry Lee Lewis's Old Sam, Hank's Tee Tot is music's equivalent of Uncle Remus, the unspoiled person who knows well because he is close to his feelings. And

Hank himself, as I have suggested, assumed Tee Tot's role for many country stars who want to claim the sincerity and spontaneity so basic in good country music. More than any other country songwriter, Hank Williams is known as one who responded directly and immediately to his experience, as one who was so spontaneous that he composed even while he was dying.

Lillie Williams encouraged that kind of story as she claimed that Hank's songs simply sprang forth. Hank himself ventured that the songs burst out of him, that sometimes they were even divinely inspired. Hank nurtured the connection to his audience when, in his preface to the second WSFA songbook, he said that many of his songs were responses to the cards and letters he received from his fans. More interesting than these claims is the mythology that flourishes around his composing; nearly every one of his best-known songs comes with at least one good story.

The myth tells us that Hank died writing that number for Audrey on his way to Canton. He supposedly had already sensed his approaching death and had recorded the premonition in "I'll Never Get out of This World Alive." The song, however, is not about last moments, but about miserably bad luck, the kind involved in being written into a will only to have a fast lawyer prove that you had never been born. But "I'll Never Get out of This World Alive" was on the charts when Hank died, and the title seemed an appropriate remark for the passing of a writer who felt so intensely.

The Nashville part of his career, we hear, began when Hank composed "Mansion on the Hill" in response to a plot given to him by Fred Rose at their first meeting. The story, denied by the Roses, has it that the composition took an unusually long thirty minutes. A menu in a Cut Off, Louisiana restaurant inspired "Jambalaya," according to one tale. According to another, the song came out of Hank's contacts with his Cajun friends on the Hadacol Caravan and was written in the back of Henry Cannon's Beechcraft Bonanza on one of Hank's returns to Nashville. The implication is that Hank suddenly came on the strange ways of the bayou folk and wrote a song about them. But we should remember that he spent some time in Shreveport and that he had written or collaborated on songs like "Bayou

Pon Pan," "Cajun Baby," and "I'm Yvonne." Moreover, we should not forget that Moon Mullican cowrote "Jambalaya."

"I Saw the Light," a song that owes something to Albert Brumley's "He Set Me Free," came to Hank when he saw the Montgomery Airport beacon, which let him know he was almost home. He may have gotten "Pan American" from the L&N Railroad, which sent so many trains through Georgiana and Greenville, but only the wildest fan would discount the obvious influence of Roy Acuff's "Wabash Cannonball" on the song. Hank seemed equally inspired when he shifted settings for another railroad tune, "California Zephyr." He wrote the funereal "Six More Miles" just after his grandmother's death. Part of "Long Gone Lonesome Blues," that number about being left and having nothing to do but watch the fish swim, came from a fishing trip with Vic McAlpin. The Kowaliga Indians, who once lived outside Montgomery near where Lake Martin is now, inspired "Kaw-Liga." And a Nashville doctor supposedly got several songs, including "You Win Again" and "Jambalaya," by demanding that Hank sit down and write six numbers as a way to sober up.

Audrey, of course, inspired plenty. She herself said that Hank wrote "Cold, Cold Heart" after he and the children had visited her in the hospital. She was angry with Hank and would not speak to him even though he gave her a fur coat on the occasion. He commented on her "cold heart" on the way home and struck up one of his best songs. "Move It on Over" came when Audrey changed the locks on him one night, leaving him to sleep in the doghouse. "Your Cheatin' Heart" materialized from a conversation about Audrey that Hank had with Billie Jean. Tales have it that the same chat produced a number for his new love, "I Could Never Be Ashamed of You," but the song is about forgiving a woman for cheating—not the best way to court fresh romance. The list could go on, and fancy would continue to dominate much of it.

As a major figure in Nashville, Hank Williams had access to plenty of material by other writers; as a beginner, he himself had sold at least one song, "I Am Waiting for the Day That Peace Will Come," to Pee Wee King for $20.[2] So he knew of the commerce between established performers and aspiring writers well before he hit the city. In Nashville, he had the good help of skilled people like Vic McAlpin and the various members of his band; Don Helms, in particular, proved to be a gifted songwriter. And, of course, Fred Rose was there to help Hank polish his compositions. One of the best documents on this relationship is a song, "Hank and Fred," done by the reorganized Drifting Cowboys. The language of the number is rough enough to keep it out of print and off wax forever, but Helms was good enough to give me a cassette copy. The song reveals the two composers at work on pieces like "Your Cheatin' Heart" and "Kaw-Liga" and then bickering over who is to get credit for them. Fred complains of how bad one of Hank's songs is and offers to do a rewrite, provided he can have half the credit. Hank says that Fred is welcome to all of it if he thinks he can sell it in the honky-tonks. On it goes, with a lot of profane banter, with the implication that the old pro was guiding a bright and rough talent and that the two were dependent on each other and willing to accept that fact.

The spirit of "Hank and Fred" is real enough. Hank was a native genius who had written some good songs before he knew Fred Rose. He was also a ninth-grade dropout who could not write music, one who both needed and could take advantage of Rose's considerable ability. We might speculate that Fred Rose would have taken more actual credit had he not been an ASCAP writer. Hank and Acuff-Rose were affiliated with BMI, and joint authorship with one writer from ASCAP and the other from BMI complicated things. But Fred Rose's reputation in Nashville is that of the patriarch, the talented and generous man who was good at helping writers develop in their own directions. Hank was fortunate to have had Fred's attention; Acuff-Rose, a profit-making enterprise, was at least as fortunate to have Hank Williams.[3]

I am not certain that tracing Fred's hand in Hank's work is either possible or entirely crucial. Chet Flippo was a little too zealous when, in *Your Cheatin' Heart*, he set out to run it all down and debunk the myth surrounding Hank's songwriting. In effect, Flippo was arguing what many knew anyway—that Hank did not find his songs under cabbage leaves. History tells us that Hank got help, however, the myth cannot be thrown out because it tells us accurately that Hank was inspired. It also tells us, more importantly than anything else, that Hank performed with such sincerity that it was easy for his audiences to believe that he had written his songs during dramatic moments in his life. He performed so convincingly that he seemed to be the sole proprietor even of songs not his own. He opened on The Grand Ole Opry with "Lovesick Blues," by Cliff Friend and Irving Mills, and he closed his recording career with "Take These Chains from My Heart," by Hy Heath and Fred Rose. As everyone knows, much of Hank Williams's music fell between the two; as most would agree, even the first and last songs have come to belong to Hank as well as to anyone. The mythology of his songwriting, then, is as much the product of his best performances as of his finest writing.

Thus, Hank Williams falls into the category with great blues performers like Billie Holiday and Janis Joplin, with great country performers like George Jones and Tammy Wynette—artists who seem inseparable from their art. As audience, we can suspend disbelief and accept what these people sing as absolute truth; or better, we can understand that they perform so well that what they sing could be true. By the same token, we can admire the passion and immediacy of Wordsworth's "Tintern Abbey" or Coleridge's "Kubla Khan" without accepting the myths that claim each poem was written in a single draft but realizing that these same myths of complete spontaneity tell us much both about the poems and the poets. Hank does not belong in the Lake Country; the simple argument is that he does belong to the old tradition of the romantic writer.

One of the great illustrations of that tradition lies in Hank's 22 December 1952 performance of "The Log Train" for neighbors and relatives in Taft Skipper's store. The song, about his father, was Hank's. It was done for people who understood it well because most of them had been associated with the Smith Lumber Company. The composer/performer died soon after the occasion. Important also is that Hank did not record the song commercially; in fact, it was lost at MGM until the Time/Life people found the demonstration record as they were preparing their issue on Hank (TLCW-01), the first in their Country and Western Classics series. The moment of this particular performance, which is historical, is complete in its representation of hard country music, a perfect closing of Hank's career.

Such is the primary significance of Hank Williams, the writer and performer, to country music. He embodied the authenticity that comes when life and art blend, an authenticity that hard country and the blues cling to, one that demands basic instruments, minimal production, and spontaneous (or apparently spontaneous) composition and performance. This authenticity may explain the popularity of The Country Music Hall of Fame manuscript exhibit that reveals the basics of any number of good country songs written on scraps of stationery and cocktail napkins. Most of these songs went through some pretty fancy and professional hands before they were recorded, but their rudiments seem to have been spontaneous. The same spontaneity is the basis of Dorothy Horstman's good book *Sing Your Heart out Country Boy*, a collection of country classics, in which each song is introduced by the story of its composition. Almost invariably, Horstman's notes connect the lyrics to some specific event or moment in the composer's life.

All of this suggests a kind of innocence, a lack of concern with fashion, an impression that the songs are being sung because they are felt and need singing. Maybe this is why a good nasal twang is so necessary to hard country—it says that the music is what it is, that it is real and untutored, without any desire to be otherwise, a point that George Jones once made with his issue, "I Am What I Am." Thus, hard country fans may be put off by Nashville's increasing sophistication, by things like its tuxedoed awards shows, which are often self-consciously imitative of more cosmopolitan show business. These same fans have to be disappointed when they hear Hank overdubbed with the strings of an MGM orchestra on recordings that completely miss the point. One even suspects that Nashville handicaps itself with the sophisticated, multitrack recording systems that can eliminate some of the authenticity that Hank and the Drifting Cowboys achieved when, all at once, they cut a number straight onto an acetate disc.

Without forgetting that Nashville's new ways produce plenty of fine music or getting too crossly conservative, I want to suggest that Hank's type of authenticity can be violated as well by performers who are too aggressive in staking their claims on hard country. I think of Barbara Mandrell, as glossy as any pop star, singing "I Was Country When Country Wasn't Cool" and of a sappy old number by Tom T. Hall, "Country Is." The bona fide hard country singer simply does not pause to define his art.

The "outlaw" performers—people like Willie Nelson, Waylon Jennings, Johnny Paycheck, and Hank Jr.—have had a lesser version of the same problem. To some extent, Hank belongs with this group in their general disregard for society's norms, and these performers are certainly eager to claim him. They sing about him regularly, in songs like Jennings's "Are You Sure Hank Done It This Way?," Paycheck's version of "Mansion on the Hill," and Hank Jr.'s "Family Tradition." Indeed, Jennings believes that Hank haunts his tour bus and keeps an extra bunk for the dead man's spirit.[4] These stars have pursued Hank for his authenticity; and because Nashville has lost touch with some of that element, several of them even moved their bases of operation out of that city. One mark of their music is its debauchery, its steady celebration of sex, drink, and drugs. One sees the connection with Hank Williams easily. But the link breaks down—and as it does, I hope it makes my point—when we realize that Hank thought he was supposed to *avoid* these things rather than recommend them. Hank's hard living would have no problem competing with that of the outlaws, but it is much more convincing because Hank did not pursue and promote it so deliberately.

Flannery O'Connor used to talk about how the South and its fiction had "manners." She referred not to courtesies, but to a distinctness, perhaps idiosyncrasy, in things like conversation, religion, politics, and so forth. This distinctness has separated the region and its fiction from the mainstream of American life. The object here is not to compare Hank Williams to O'Connor, but to say that hard country has a similar set of manners: things like its considerable emotionalism, its themes, its sincerity, its rough-edged characters, and maybe even its nasal twang. Like the South itself, the fiction and the music are being diminished steadily as major currents of national life pull at them. But stubborn types, like O'Connor from one art form and Williams from another, are appealing for their resistance to conformity and strident commercialism.

Appropriate recognition does not always come to these kinds of artists. Society has a way of sweeping by them. But when the mainstream does discover them, it seems to cherish them all the more, perhaps because we enjoy the sense of discovery or perhaps because we like to see the apparently insignificant character have his day. And the appreciation becomes especially sweet when it has not been sought out. One takes pleasure in watching a writer like O'Connor—who seemed not to worry much that the reading public looked upon her as a quaint, if not bizarre, Southern lady—become a mainstay of American letters. Long-term fans of country music can take a similar pleasure in knowing that the general public now seems to realize that hard country music is not just something to burn tires by. Without compromising, without ever becoming anything except the boisterous country boy that he had always been, Hank Williams certainly gained the attention of mainstream America.

I think this is why the stories about outdoing Bob Hope or putting Milton Berle in his place have become such popular parts of the biography. The once obscure Hank Williams was overtaking two of popular culture's most highly regarded stars, and country fans take fierce pleasure in the triumph. I also believe that this was the importance of Hank's being invited to Hollywood. The invitation was a sign of his considerable appeal. That he turned down one contract and botched another, apparently by insulting Dore Schary, makes the story even better. Hank just did not seem too worried about promoting himself. His alcoholism may explain part of his lack of interest, but nonetheless the image of Hank as a country original who did not care about Hollywood glitz is vivid. Whether intentional or not, avoiding film was probably smart; Hank might have made a lot of money, but he would have sacrificed much of his authenticity had he become a singing cowboy on a Hollywood horse.

Popular music was more successful than Hollywood in its notice of Hank Williams. The many pop covers include those by Marty Gold, Connie Francis, Del Shannon, Buddy Greco, Connie Stevens, and even Spike Jones. BMI gave pop awards to "Cold, Cold Heart," "I'm So Lonesome I Could Cry," "Jambalaya," and "Your Cheatin' Heart." Tony Bennett made a career with his million-selling version of "Cold, Cold Heart." Frankie Laine and Jo Stafford did well with "Hey Good Lookin'," and Stafford became known by her rendition of "Jambalaya." I am sure that Rosemary Clooney could explained what "Why Don't You Love Me?" meant to her career. Rhythm and blues man Ray Charles surely understands the importance of "Your Cheatin' Heart." And if Perry Como put Hank on television as a rural oddity in the early 1950s, it was probably Hank and country music that brought the crooner to the South in the early 1960s to wax a Nashville version of "Dream on Little Dreamer."

A particular irony here is that rock, the music that did so much to push country aside in the 1950s and 1960s, made good use of some of Hank's material. Bill Haley, the first white rocker, got to jumping with "Too Many Parties and Too Many Pals." The song was not Hank's, but it was Hank's 1950 version of it that the Haley was trading on. Haley had been a country picker—one who called himself "Yodeling" Bill Haley and who had called his band The Four Aces of Western Swing before he dubbed them The Comets.[5] He was sacrificing a small country career to bolt toward rock and roll, and he was making use of Hank in the switch. In 1952, the year after Hank's "Cold, Cold Heart" had been such a hit, Haley shamelessly thought up a tune called "Icy Heart." Thus, Hank played a part in the founding of rock and roll, a part that would get support when the Pearls did "Your Cheatin' Heart," when Fats Domino did "Jambalaya," and when a wild country rocker named Jerry Lee Lewis started pounding his way to the big time with "You Win Again."

Robert Shelton says accurately that Hank "was the first country song writer to have become solidly entrenched with the pop singers of Tin Pan Alley, almost single-handedly bringing about the union of pop and country which followed his death."[6] My point, though, is this: In spite of all of his appeal to broad audiences, all of his potential for pop stardom, Hank Williams did not cross over after his songs. Again and again while doing this research, I have heard the story of Hank stopping to play Tony Bennett's "Cold, Cold Heart" on the jukebox. The story is such a good one because it indicates the willingness of the country singer and songwriter to be audience for his own songs after they had made their way into the world of pop music. But Hank himself just did not change.

I have to keep in mind, of course, that Hank's career was extremely brief and not very well designed. Had he straightened up and lived longer, he might have fallen among smooth promoters and turned up with a new hairstyle, a saxophone, and a less nasal sound. But I doubt it. Hank felt that he was doing all right, that tampering with a good thing was pointless. We can be glad that he did not make movies, and we can be just as glad that Hank Williams did not become a Haley rocker or a Como/Bennett crooner, that his authenticity survived as long as he did. If we are concerned that some of his numbers drifted into the music that was going to stall country for a decade or so, we might enjoy knowing that Hank's infiltrations of pop and rock probably helped broaden the tastes of a nation eager to listen to country music today.

THE LOVER

The good Calvinistic South has always known how to enjoy its despair. A war lost to the North, hard work, and some poverty are not bad topics for sweet misery. But no subject suits the purposes better than broken love, which proves that even the best thing we have cannot survive in this world.

Without much doubt, failed romance is the major subject of country music, and country fans have long heard plenty about it. The Carter family dealt with the theme early on in numbers like "Wildwood Flower" and "I'm Thinkin' Tonight of My Blue Eyes." Jimmy Davis and Charles Mitchell produced a classic in "You Are My Sunshine." Jimmie Rodgers sang about being wrecked by a woman in his first blue yodel, "T For Texas." Bob Wills's "San Antonio Rose" still gets attention, as does Bill Monroe's "Kentucky Waltz." And the pace hardly slackens when we turn to the contemporary country scene.

In her essay on the subject, Dorothy Horstman quotes Webb Pierce: "It's different things that make a song a hit. One of the things is you sing about the things they think about most, but don't talk about. That becomes an emotional outlet for the people, and they feel they have a friend in the song." Horstman sees World War II as an important factor here because it separated so many lovers and because it gave independence to many women by sending them to work.[7] The war brought the era of the "Dear John" letter, and it brought some sad hits like Ted Daffan's "Born to Lose" and Ernest Tubb's "Walking the Floor over You."

Hank Williams, his career taking hold as the war came to an end, was certainly ready to pitch in on the subject, ready to make love-gone-wrong part of the grain of country music. One of country's great scenes has him leaning into a microphone and breaking his voice over a song of shattered love, a song powerful on its own but even more powerful because looming behind it were Hank's crazy romances. "Lovesick" Hank Williams knew what he was singing about; and with his melancholy streak, he brought the music a pathos especially appealing to those whose love had been threatened or broken. The result, as Horstman puts it, is that "Williams remains to this day the most sympathetic and successful figure in the musical expression of unrequited love."[8]

Hank came to the theme without much trouble. His mother had shown him something of the comings and goings of love while he was still a child. Lillie and Lon were not the best match. Chet Flippo has them slugging it out in *Your Cheatin' Heart.* And though Flippo tends to exaggerate, Lillie seems to have shed little grief when Lon left in 1929 for his long stays in VA hospitals. She evidently received some male attention in his absence and made no real effort to retrieve him from his sickbed. Certainly, she did not welcome Lon to her home in Montgomery when he showed up after many years of hospitalization. No one seems certain of the number of Lillie's husbands, and records are difficult to find; friends and relatives have told me that "several" plighted their troth to Lillie and received some rough treatment in return. Wherever they are, W. W. Stone and the Mr. Bozard—not to mention Lon—could testify to that.

Like his mother, Hank seemed to require romance. He learned from her that it rarely went smoothly and that its terms generally were dictated by women. Audrey reinforced these lessons. She had moved into Lillie's boardinghouse while her husband, Erskine Guy, was overseas; ironically, Guy might have been the perfect audience for those songs of broken love that Hank was to write and sing so well. Audrey may or may not have been on Hank's trail when she arrived at Lillie's, but she was to be after him soon. And it seems that she knew how to get into his tough heart quickly. She became his lover at home, his partner on the road.

If that situation sounds ideal, it was not. Hank and Audrey never had it easy. Lillie stretches things in her book, once more, when she says that "You could know just how Hank and Audrey were getting along at all times by listening to his latest hits on records and radio."[9] Neither Hank nor the media was always agile enough to keep up with the turnings of that love, but Audrey did generously supply the tension that seemed to inspire Hank's writing. Life with Hank left no shortage of things to quarrel over. Lillie's boardinghouse was no honeymoon suite. Audrey was frustrated, a would-be star who could not carry a tune. Hank got lots of attention from other women, and rather obviously, he drank too much. Audrey was not far from her parents, and she often furled the flag and left Lillie's for home. Hank's job with the Alabama Drydock and Shipbuilding Company in Mobile made for similar charges and retreats on his part.

The entire affair was impetuous. They got married in a filling station during a road trip, and they fought on many others. Supposedly, one such tiff had Hank pulling Audrey out of the car by her hair to leave her by the roadside only to find her waiting for the crew at the next joint that sold Falstaff. Obviously, the 1948 divorce was extemporaneous. The terms of the split were cordial enough to allow the conception of Hank Jr. The Opry and the accompanying travel meant more separations, probably more infidelities, and certainly more jealousies. All of this led to the real and permanent divorce of 1952, a split that marked the end of Hank's career about as well as his being fired from the Opry.

Friends of the couple in both Nashville and Montgomery almost invariably say that Hank and Audrey loved each other deeply, but just could not get along. In fact, Audrey's extra men were enough to lead some to speculate about the paternity of Hank Jr. Hank did his part in betrayal, and apparently Bobbie Jett and Billie Jean were only two among many. One wonders why Hank never got a song out of the occasion when those two women collided at Lillie's in the fall of 1952.

The stage weddings to Billie Jean were fundraisers. Hank needed cash, and he was going commercial with some private business, no doubt. He sang, got married, and made nearly $15,000 in the bargain. But the moment has some symbolic value as well. Singing love songs—"Jambalaya" was the hit of the festivity—and getting married suggest something about Hank's sense of weaving his life with his music. The audience knew the whole story—of Audrey and Hank Jr. in Nashville and Hank and his new *ma chere amieo* in Shreveport. Some people were happy to see Hank have new romance. Many more just could not believe that Hank and Audrey were finally finished. Like Hank's good Montgomery friends, Braxton and Ola Schuffert, they were convinced that Hank was going to straighten himself out and work his way back to Audrey. Some believed that Hank invited Audrey to the wedding, met her at the airport, and then sent her back to Nashville when she refused to reconcile. Another story has him totally ineffective as Billie Jean's lover; another has Hank desperately trying to call Audrey during that last trip to Canton in 1952. Fans just would not give up on the drama of Hank and Audrey.

The drama would not have been so sharply etched if Hank had not sung about it with such feeling. His response to experience seemed direct, and it was always simple. He spent little time developing the elaborate comparisons that country music sometimes stretches for. "Your Cheatin' Heart," a landmark for Hank Williams and for country music, is almost completely unadorned. This directness heightened Hank's considerable gift for sharp images. The sleepless nights of the treacherous lover in "Your Cheatin' Heart" are as vivid as the memory of a happy past that steals through the mind of a man who sees his woman with a new lover in "I Can't Help It (If I'm Still in Love with You)." Hank's "I'm So Lonesome I Could Cry" contains one of the most striking images in country music as it tells how the silence of a falling star lights up the night. Hank might not have been interested in my point, but his image is synesthetic, the kind that mixes the senses. We get one image of sound, another of sight as quietness brightens the dark. The two images do not make sense together, except that the night is often quiet when we see falling stars and we are often lonely when we stare into the dark. The simplicity of the lines keeps the image from seeming self-conscious just as it makes it so startling, so profoundly lonesome.

Hank made some other contributions to country's sad love songs. He must have been one of the first to hint at divorce when he recommended splitting up rather than putting up with half-hearted love in "Why Should We Try Anymore?" But he did not usually have such an easy solution to problems of the heart. His best songs involved potentially fine romance that, for one reason or another, does not work out. He sang less about love that has ended and much more about one-sided love, the kind that lingers even when it cannot possibly be fulfilled. The result was a pathos and self-pity that Hank mastered; with the help of fiddler Jerry Rivers and steel guitarist Don Helms, he could practically get a tear on command. The early number, "Mansion on the Hill," works at the idea as it reveals the poor boy who can never have his rich girl because of the obvious social differences. The boy, pining away in his cabin in the valley, simply could not miss with an audience sensitive to snobbery.

The pathetic lover, who offers more affection than his beloved can bear, turns up over and over. If she could love him only "Half as Much," he could be happy. His love goes beyond hers in "I Can't Help It (If I'm Still in Love with You)." "Take These Chains from My Heart" may suggest divorce again as it speaks of losing faith and needing escape, but, because it discusses lingering heartaches, it has the fine ambiguity of wanting to be rid of a woman and wanting to keep her at the same time. "You Win Again" catches the same ambiguity. She abuses him, and he should leave; but he just cannot stop his passion. Hank found more pathos in Claude Boone's "Wedding Bells," a hit second only to "Lovesick Blues" in 1949. Here the lover watches his love marry another. Hank did it again in Leon Payne's "They'll Never Take Her Love from Me," where, to prove love, the singer steps aside so his beloved can marry another. And she does, leaving his testimony of affection to feed on itself. "I'd Still Want You" is about pretending not to care, about not letting friends know just how much one loves an abusive woman. In "My Heart Would Know," Hank could feign that his affection had died, but his crying heart would know the truth.

Hank's best expressions of love being hopeless in spite of great potential probably lie in "Your Cheatin' Heart" and "Cold, Cold Heart." In the former, the lover seems to be having some revenge on a faithless woman as he imagines the sleepless nights she will get for doing him wrong. But then he gives his true emotions away by admitting that his nights are just as restless as he imagines hers to be—the subtle indication being that most of the misery belongs to him. In "Cold, Cold Heart," Hank loves intensely, but his beloved has been hurt before and does not trust his affection. The more he tries to express his love, the more suspicious of him she becomes. Because she has been hurt, she needs the love that she just cannot accept.

The song tells all about the sadly ironic view of love that dominated the life and work of Hank Williams.

Thus, love for Hank and for more than a few in his audiences ran its absurd course. Through Hank, country came to work out one of its sustaining themes—the perplexing business of lovers and beloveds, of needing love and rejecting it all at the same time. Whatever the love song, Hank always seemed to be indicating that he and Audrey could have been great lovers had they been able to stay in the same household long enough. The good fan has to see Hank behind country's great songs of lost love—behind numbers like "The Tennessee Waltz" that Patti Page made famous, George Morgan's "Candy Kisses," Bob and John Wills's "Faded Love," the synoptic "Dear John," Barbara Mandrell's "'Till You're Gone," and George Jones's "He Stopped Loving Her Today." And Hank and Audrey practically have haunted the stages occupied by great duos like George Jones and Tammy Wynette, Conway Twitty and Loretta Lynn, Dolly Parton and Porter Waggoner, perhaps even David Frizzell and Shelley West—all of them fully aware of what Hank's authenticity has meant to country music.

SIN AND SALVATION

Hank heard much of the music of his early years at Mount Olive Baptist Church, where his mother played the organ. The story goes that he sat with Lillie at the instrument. If this makes Hank seem remarkably pious, we might note other gossip around Georgiana and Mount Olive to the effect that Hank was a bit of a rapscallion who called for supervision while his mother was occupied with the church's music—thus his perch in the front. Whether for discipline or devotion, Hank was prominent in church in those first years, and Mount Olive's congregation has memorialized with a plaque the little wooden bench he stood on to sing his first songs.

Hank's musical heritage was not all sacred, though. His aunt, Mrs. McNeil, no doubt taught Hank some hymns when he lived with her family during the school year of 1934—1935. But the lumber camp that was his home that year taught him plenty of tunes that got no one into heaven. Tee Tot must have known some sacred numbers, but he was a man of the street and had a few notions about the secular world. By the time Hank arrived in Montgomery in 1935, ready to start his own career, he had a grasp of both kinds of music and an awareness that sincerity carried a blues number as well as it carried hymns. Hank put that awareness to work on the radio shows and in the schoolhouse concerts, which allowed a certain amount of rowdiness but insisted on a sacred closing.

But Hank was to make his way in the honky-tonks fairly soon; and the joints, which had been given such a fine air of evil by Prohibition, did not make much room for spirituality. In trying to define honky-tonk music, Nick Tosches talks about the "small-group sound that developed in redneck bars" and then cites the "lyrics of sex and whiskey." To give this music its setting, Tosches quotes Al Dexter, who defined the honky-tonks as "these beer joints up and down the road where girls jump in cars and so on."[10] By talent and temperament, Hank Williams was well suited to the honky-tonks. As Peter Guralnick puts it, "Unless you were a schooled musician and could read and play with some of the larger groups, the small honky-tonk bands were the path of least resistance, and what they were playing then, same as now, was boogie music for dancing with a country-oriented beat and instrumentation."[11] Hank served much of his apprenticeship in these places, working there steadily from about 1938 until he hit The Grand Ole Opry in 1949, and he made plenty more stops among them after he was an Opry regular.

Much of his music was for or from those scenes. In the little known "I've Been down That Road Before," Hank laments the risks of being a smart aleck, the type he tended to be at times, among the rowdy boys. He complains of some knots on his bald head and of some missing teeth before describing a time when he was so beat up that his mother did not recognize him after he was hauled home. A more memorable song, "Honky Tonk Blues," follows suit as Hank sings about leaving a good country home to hit the night spots of the city. In the end, he claims to have had enough and to be heading back to his daddy's farm.

Not all of Hank's juke-joint songs come to such moral conclusions. In "Honky Tonkin'," a man invites someone else's wife to party. If she has some money, he claims, he can show her some wicked places. "Hey Good Lookin'" is from the same cloth. The singer attempts to lure the lady from her stove, from her good domestic life, to cook up something with him, something, one assumes, having little to do with fat back and green beans. Hank offers her no commitment beyond $2, plenty of soda, and some dancing. He is just as blunt in "I'll Be a Bachelor Till I Die," where he gallantly offers to hold the girl's hand, pet her when she cries, let her cool him with her fan (that great Southern euphemism for ardency in polite parlor courtship), and take her honk-tonkin'. Marriage, as the title makes plain, is not part of the program.

Hank even found ways to get hound dogs, those critters that have always fascinated country, into his honky-tonk tunes. "Move It on Over" is the classic about the locked-out lover sleeping in the doghouse. "Homesick" concerns the errant lover who jokingly says he will do anything to get back into his lover's house; if she wants a new dog, he claims, he will learn to bark. "Howlin' at the Moon" is even more whimsical as it describes a man going happily after a coy woman. She has him so confused that he wears socks for neckties, tries to eat steaks with a spoon, and, of course, howls at the moon. In fact, he claims to have become the best hound in the county for want of her.

"Long Gone Lonesome Blues" is not quite as mournful as its title suggests, and the number went well with the rowdy crowds. Here Hank talks about being so lonesome that he tries to drown himself. Fortunately, the river was dry. Hank would break his voice over the refrain, creating a kind of witty despair that was not to be taken too seriously. In "Why Don't You Love Me?" he just cannot understand why the beloved is so cold; he allows that he is as handsome as ever, the same trouble she has always known, and that he just cannot fathom the cooling of her passion. "No, Not Now" comes from the old jokes about wives resisting their husbands. They make their men wait during courtship, and for some strange reason they make them wait even after they are married.

This jesting at the passionate lover made Hank's honky-tonk music unique because the genre has often focused on lost lovers drinking away their miseries. Classics like "City Lights," "Lost Highway," "There Stands the Glass," "The Wild Side of Life," "Honky Tonk Angel," "After the Fire Is Gone," and "She's Acting Single (I'm Drinking Doubles)" are typical examples. Bad romance becomes an excuse for drinking and running around. Hank's songs, remarkably, did not mix the issues. Usually, broken love was just plain grief, whereas drinking and carousing were just good fun, a separate matter altogether. The separation effectively marked the apparent sincerity of Hank's approach to love; its twistings and turnings were not just a reason for more drink. And those deeply sad and lonely love songs set up perfectly the happy music he loved to play.

The raucous music could turn his concerts into blasts, and stories of his performances are legendary. Perhaps the best known of those occasions involved his attempt to sing "My Bucket's Got a Hole in It" on The Grand Old Opry. Hank had scheduled the number, but Opry officials balked when they realized that it included the word "beer." Hank could sing the song, they decided, but the "beer" had to go. Supposedly, the star complained that he did not see why he could not say "beer" on stage since he was going on full of the elixir anyway. Finally, Hank obliged the officials, dropped the "beer," and went out to wail about a leaking bucket that kept him from buying "buttermilk." The crowd, familiar with the song and with wicked Hank as well, loved it. A Dallas audience waited for him until after midnight and then cheered a tipsy Hank when he opened the show with "good morning." Another crowd may have been angry enough when he stood them up in Richmond, but they were back the next day to get their money's worth during that show in which he made fun of reviewer Edith Lindeman by dedicating "Mind Your Own Business" to her. In fact, Hank practically became a hero for being drunk and missing a show. The "bad boy" was just a part of Hank and his music, and his audiences seemed to understand that in his rowdy ways he was just showing them what he was. George Jones enjoys Hank's privilege even today.

Hank was just as real in his religion. For all of his iniquity, he never shook off those beginnings back at the Mount Olive Baptist Church. The three-year-old child sang his first notes there, and the adult man returned to a similar setting just before he died. Hank and Billie Jean went to the Chapman Methodist Church with Taft and Erleen Skipper on the night of 21 December 1952. Hank sang with the congregation, but he turned down the invitation to perform individually even though he was willing to sing for the same friends and acquaintances the next morning in Taft's store. He may have been too weary to go before the Methodists that night, but Erleen told me that Hank did not feel that his recent life allowed him to lead church music. It is easy to believe that he was so serious about his religion, at least at the moment.

Hank knew the reality of "I Saw the Light" as well as that of "Honky Tonkin'." The latter may have dominated, but a full 20 percent of the songs he wrote are sacred. Apparently, Hank had felt some urge to moralize when he took the persona of "Luke the Drifter." Numbers like "Pictures from Life's Other Side" tell us that people who seem to be bad can have good hearts, and "Be Careful of the Stones That You Throw" contains another warning of hypocrisy. Hank did fourteen Luke sides; he got composer credit for half of them, while several other hands, mainly those of Fred Rose, were in the others. However, composition is not the issue here because the lyrics of these pieces are unimpressive. But in performance, Hank gave Luke a convincing sincerity. In an excellent 1997 summary of these takes, Thomas Wilmeth compares Luke's regionalisms with Hank's own speech patterns. His point is that the song/recitations were so sincere and convincing because Hank infused his persona, Luke, with his own language. Wilmeth also notes importantly that Hank was "unapologetic and seemingly instinctive about presenting this regional tone."[12] With "Lovesick Blues," Hank had shown how he could take possession of a song, and he did much the same thing with the Luke numbers. At the same time, he expanded his range, proving that the Hank Williams who could sing wrenching love songs, hot juke-joint numbers, and sincere religious songs could handle even Luke's moralistic parables.

Some of Hank's religious music is fairly standard. "The Angel of Death," "Are You Walking and A-Talking for the Lord?," "Calling You," "Jesus Is Calling," "Ready to Go Home," "When the Book of Life Is Read," and "I'm Gonna Sing" are traditional in their sentiments about whether we are prepared to die and what heaven will be like. The song "A Home in Heaven" concerns those who build good homes here without preparing for one above. "A House of Gold" and "Wealth Won't Save Your Soul" are similar in their comments on materialism. "Last Night I Dreamed of Heaven" is about meeting loved ones above. Several of Hank's hymns, however, are truly striking. "How Can You Refuse Him Now?," "Jesus Died for Me," and "We're Getting Closer to the Grave Each Day" are all simple, but each deals vividly with the crucifixion. Each song details Christ on the cross, the nailed hands, and the crown of thorns, as sinners are called to realize the importance of Christian sacrifice. "Jesus Remembered Me" is just as graphic as it depicts the lost sinner who finally looks up and is greatly surprised to find that Jesus recognizes him.

The easy acceptance of the details of biblical history and the sincere rendering of them are the marks of Hank's great sacred songs, the marks of most good hymns. These songs bring the events of salvation out of what may seem to be the vague past into the distinct present, thus connecting directly the sinner and his salvation. Few hymns do this better than "I Saw the Light," a convincing song that links Christ's healing of the blind man with His healing of the modern sinner. Hank captured here the full meaning of the biblical story, and he presented it simply as history, without the sermonizing that might have gone into it. The hymn becomes particularly moving when we know its stories, the one about Hank seeing the airport beacon that meant he was almost home, the other about how, so deep in his problems late in life, Hank would not sing the hymn with Minnie Pearl because, as he put it, "There ain't no light. It's all dark."[13]

In spite of Hank's gift for sacred music, I think Lillie Williams was wrong to suggest in her book that her son "was a sort of preacher at heart." Mothers can be forgiven that sort of thing. But Al Bock made the same error, at greater length, in *I Saw the Light: The Gospel Life of Hank Williams*, in which he argues that Hank was a major religious figure. Also, Jay Caress over-christianized Hank in *Hank Williams: Country Music's Tragic King*. Hank was not a pious man trying to push aside a corrupt world; he pursued sin more than he pursued Jesus. But guilt seemed to overtake him from time to time, and he was just great at generating the tension between Saturday night hell raising and Sunday morning piety.

Hank Williams brought that tension to a Grand Ole Opry that had been intent on preserving a happier view of human nature. Generally, the show's subjects had been the wholesomeness of dogs, biscuits, work, trains, trucks, and religion. Well-scrubbed families might stand in line for a day at the ticket window of Ryman Auditorium, formerly a church, without even imagining a riot. Performers appeared to be nearly as wholesome—and if they did drink and carouse a bit, they did so out of sight. An old-time group like The Fruit Jar Drinkers had actually felt compelled to change their reckless name to the Dixie Sacred Singers when they recorded religious numbers. When Roy Acuff brought Rachel Veach into his band, he got considerable mail complaining about a woman traveling with all those men. Acuff solved the problem by turning band member Beecher Kirby into Bashful Brother Oswald to suggest that Rachel was family, her virtue quite safe after all.

Opry officials did not know what to do with Hank Williams, except to try to keep him sober and to keep him from singing "beer" on stage. He was obviously a threat to the hallowed grounds of Nashville. In their wisdom—or in their eagerness to seize hot property—they let him into the Ryman for a few years until he became too outrageous to keep. While he was there, Hank Williams taught the Opry to allow a little misbehavior in its music, if, at least at first, only to point out the wages of sin.

The idea certainly took hold. Misbehavior became a part of country, and generally it has been tempered with some kind of disapproval or punishment. We were to see many legacies of old profane and sacred Hank Williams. Kenny Rogers's Ruby did take her love to town. Helen Cornelius and Jim Ed Brown sang of spreading blankets on the ground. Dolly Parton became a sex symbol, one who splits out of her dresses as she goes up to receive another country award, a country singer who would star in the film version of *The Best Little Whorehouse in Texas*. But when we look past the sensual, we find a backdrop of morality. Ruby, as she takes her love elsewhere, is betraying a badly wounded veteran of Vietnam, in a sense betraying America itself with her loose ways. Helen and Jim Ed could spread their blankets because they are married, at least in the song, just a spunky middle-aged couple trying to recapture some old passion. And because of her giggles and taffeta, the vampish Dolly Parton, so oblivious to her own cleavage, seems capable of believing that the stork brings babies. She and Porter Waggoner knew that they would get caught if they kept meeting at "The Dark End of the Street." George Jones and Tammy Wynette sang flirtatiously that "God's Gonna Get 'Cha for That." And we understand that Shel Silverstein's queen of the Silver Dollar was really unhappy in spite of all the action.

Sin and Salvation got one of its major country expressions in *Hee Haw*, that long-running television show of the 1970s. The program, which became nearly as monumental as the Opry itself, brought on all sorts of flesh, most of it concentrated in what was known as the All Jug Band, a group of buxom females who barely managed tunes by puffing on various jugs and jars. But *Hee Haw* always closed on a religious note, clean overalls and a good a cappella version of some familiar four-square hymn, something that allowed an audience, tempted by the flesh, to regather itself and sing along.

Among the "outlaws," even Willie Nelson himself seems capable of repentance, probably because he is likely to follow songs like "Whiskey

River" or "Bloody Mary Morning" with a sanctified rendering of "Amazing Grace." His film *Honeysuckle Rose* allowed a good bit of hard drinking (some of it done by drivers weaving down the highway in a bus), a good bit of womanizing, and the feature attraction—Willie seducing the twenty-year-old daughter of his best friend. The film might have needed an R rating if wholesomeness did not envelop the licentiousness. It included many happy family scenes, sad partings, and touching reunions as Willie and his band begin and end their tours. Finally, the wayward hero is home, chastened a bit but forgiven, convinced that he loves only his wife, the fairly sexy Dyan Cannon. All came to be right with the world; titillation had been served while pious morality won out.

Country music went on to eliminate much of the moral tension that Hank Williams brought to it. The music's persistent innuendo—the references to sex, booze, and drugs—does not call for so much repentance today. Although Hank's life and music foreshadowed much of this liberation, I want to say that he did a much better job of it than most of those who followed him. The deep sincerity that he projected defeated any potential for hypocrisy. And I will always believe that the best and most important country show would have Hank Williams bending into "I'm So Lonesome I Could Cry," "Honky Tonkin'," and "I Saw the Light."

THE SHRINE

Many years ago, the Nashville *Tennessean* reported a strange tale. During the television taping of "That Good Ole Nashville Music," Gary Gentry was singing his new song, "The Ride." The number tells of a hitchhiker on his way to Nashville who gets picked up by a man in a Cadillac. As they approach the city, the driver turns around to head for his home in Alabama. He lets his passenger out and asks him to call him "Hank." When Gentry sang that last "Hank," the lights all over Opryland went out. Electricians found a burned open switch. Gentry, along with everyone else on hand, was fast to claim the electrical failure as Hank's guiding hand in the song.[14] Perhaps the freakish, or staged, moment that supplied such good publicity for a young singer tells us something of the pervasiveness of Hank's spirit in Nashville.

A sign from Hank seems capable of making a career because the country music world simply venerates him. It has given him all of its significant prizes, and a *Down Beat* poll has shown Hank Williams to be the "most popular country and western singer of all time." In 1961, Hank joined Jimmie Rodgers and Fred Rose as the first members of the Country Music Hall of Fame. By 1969, "Your Cheatin' Heart" had its millionth broadcast performance, and BMI recognized the occasion with a "Special Citation of Achievement." Hank's "Jambalaya" received the same citation in 1971. Long before Gary Gentry got his break at Opryland, country singers were making tributes to Hank. Elvis may have generated more souvenirs and more printed words, but Hank Williams has inspired more music—from his own kind, the professionals who understand his impact best—than any other American singer. The long list of tributes could start with songs like Jimmy Logsdon's "Hank Sings the Blues No More," Arthur Smith's "In Memory of Hank Williams," and Ernest Tubb's "Hank, It Will Never Be the Same without You." It would run on through Waylon Jennings's "Are You Sure Hank Done It This Way?," Mike Cross's "Thanks Hank," Travis Pritchett's "Hank's Home Town," Bob McDill's "Good Old Boys Like Me" (the good old boys are Hank and Tennessee Williams), Kris Kristofferson's "If You Don't Like Hank Williams," and Paul Craft's "Hank Williams, You Wrote My Life." Charlie Pride, a black country star, sang "There's a Little Bit of Hank in Me."

Celebrating and selling Hank Williams has grown into its own industry, and Hank's music is so prominent that it has been the subject of parody. In a piece called "Hippie Boy" by Chris Hillman and Gram Parsons, The Flying Burrito Brothers sent up "The Funeral," one of the Luke the Drifter numbers. Hank's Luke speaks of coming across the Savannah funeral of a black child; the piece is condescending and sentimental as he discusses the general ignorance and simplicity of the black people gathered to mourn the passing. Luke goes on to suggest that, in spite of the boy's color, the child was good and is with God. The Hillman-Parsons version is about the death of a little drug courier who, on a mission for a few dollars, had tried to eat the drugs when he got caught. As unseemly as he may be, he, too, is with God, long hair and all. Roy Blount also pokes gently at the industry with his "Why Ain't I Half as Good as Old Hank (Since I'm Feeling All Dead Anyway)?"[15]

Hank Williams impersonators come and go, and Hank Williams festivals thrive. Peter Bogdanovich's movie *The Last Picture Show* marked an entire era with a sound track made up basically of Hank's songs. Fans still buy millions of dollars worth of his music. They flock from long distances to see his things at the Country Music Hall of Fame and in the Hank Williams Museum in Montgomery. They visit his grave in that city's Oakwood Cemetery Annex—a graveyard marked by a sign with a drawing of Hank's boots and guitar, the only necessary directions—to such an extent that caretakers had to replace the grass around the grave with artificial turf. Taft and Erleen Skipper told me that they had to sleep with the phone off the hook because of so many calls about their famous cousin.

Hank came to Nashville at the right time. Country music was quickly getting popular. It had its own recording experts at Castle, its publisher in Acuff-Rose, its protector in BMI. Hank thrived with the industry and died just as rock and roll was ready to vibrate across the nation. But to see him simply as the product of history would be a mistake, for he shaped and substantiated country music at least as much as it shaped and substantiated him. Hank Williams was a natural, a unique combination of writer and performer, who either initiated or magnified the basic characteristics of a genre that was just realizing itself as a phenomenon of American culture. Because of his particular life and talent, Hank Williams was able to show country music the importance of authenticity more dramatically than any writer and performer before or since. He articulated more clearly than anyone the full emotional range of broken romance. Then he cut his melancholy love songs with some loose, juke-joint tunes to prove to country that plain wholesomeness just was not enough, that human experience involved a little more than home cooking. And he tempered it all with some deep religious feelings that gave his life and his music a tension irresistible to fans who knew him well. Hank Williams came and went with one of country music's great moments. This great period was bordered roughly by World War II and Elvis's start with Sun Records in 1954, or just as well by Hank's arrival in Nashville in 1946 and his death in 1953.

3

The Resources

The primary resource, obviously, is the music itself. And despite Hank's very brief studio time, the legacy is plentiful and easily available. Hank Williams began his recording career in Nashville on 11 December 1946 in Studio D of Castle Recording Company. He cut four of his own songs for Sterling Records that day; the most famous one was "When God Comes and Gathers His Jewels." The Oklahoma Wranglers, known later as the Willis Brothers and identified on the Sterling records as the Country Boys, did the backup music. Sterling had Hank back for four more sides and paid him another $82.50 on 13 February 1947.

That spring, Hank began recording for MGM, and he stayed with the company for the rest of his career. Backup men on the early sessions included Tommy Jackson, Chubby Wise, Dale Potter, Don Davis, Jerry Byrd, Jack Shook, Zeb Turner, Ernie Newton, Fred Rose, Owen Bradley, Bill Drake, Louie Innis, and Brownie Reynolds. The most enduring version of the Drifting Cowboys evolved in 1949 and had Don Helms on steel guitar, Jerry Rivers on fiddle, and Hillous Butrum on bass. That band recorded with Hank for the first time on 9 January 1950. From then on, they were his standard backup group, although they were supplemented by various studio musicians, especially rhythm guitarist Jack Shook. In the summer of 1950, Sammy Pruett replaced McNett and Howard (Cedric Rainwater) Watts replaced Butrum. Hank usually played an open, rhythm guitar. He and the band did almost all of their recording with Nashville's Castle Recording Company, which had studios at WSM and in the Tulane Hotel, but they did two important sessions in the Herzog Studios in Cincinnati (22 December 1948 and 30 August 1949).

After about thirty-five sessions and just over ninety commercial recordings, Hank cut his last songs, "I Could Never Be Ashamed of You," "Your Cheatin' Heart," "Kaw-Liga," and "Take These Chains from My Heart." That remarkable last session was recorded on 23 September 1952. Hank was dead a few months later, and MGM was without one of its best properties. A fine songwriter and performer, who should have had another forty years or more, was gone.

MGM was resourceful in handling the Williams catalog, however. Hank had cut any number of demonstration records, some of them in Montgomery and others in Fred Rose's attic studio. They were safe in the MGM vault. These recordings were not always finished products, but many of them were quite good. Besides, because they were by Hank Williams, they would sell. The company issued some sixty-five of these nonsession cuts, about two-thirds of them with overdubbed backup music supporting Hank and his guitar. No doubt, their steady appearance on the market fueled the rumor that Hank Williams was not dead after all.

MGM would find additional resources. The company received cuts from the Armed Forces Radio Services (AFRS) transcriptions of The Grand Ole Opry, and they took cuts from the eight sixteen-inch 33s that Hank had done for the LeBlanc Corporation in October 1949. MGM, of course, collected various records into sets. The company issued 78 cuts as 45s, then the 45s went onto 33 LPs. The modern buyer should note that Hank himself barely knew what a 33 LP was and that he was dead long before anyone had even thought of a compact disc.

MGM executive Jim Vienneau, the nephew of Frank Walker, gave things another twist when he started elaborate overdubbing of Hank's work. He was not applying the standard small-band music that had gone behind many of the nonsession recordings. Rather, Vienneau brought orchestras to Hank; he put multiple strings behind him or superimposed Hank Jr.'s voice on that of his father's. Thus, we got to hear something that never happened— Hank and Hank Jr. singing "My Son Calls Another Man Daddy." Vienneau's process was not simple because the original cuts had gone directly onto acetate discs, not onto the multiple tracks of today's recording studio. With separate tracks, one can simply withdraw a voice or an instrument and substitute another. With the old discs, however, the various voices and instruments were inseparable and permanent because they had all been recorded at the same moment. Overdubbing them meant drowning out particular sounds, superimposing new sounds onto old recordings, and keeping an orchestra in sync with a record being played over a studio sound system. Most serious Hank Williams fans consider such overdubbing a desecration. I join them in that feeling.

The first major discography of Hank Williams was done by Jerry Rivers for his *Hank Williams: From Life to Legend*. Rivers cites each record and the songs on it and ends with a list of records in tribute to Hank. Almost the same discography appeared at the end of the Ballantine edition of Roger M. Williams's *Sing a Sad Song: The Life of Hank Williams*; at the end of Al Bock's *I Saw the Light: The Gospel Life of Hank Williams*; and at the end of Jay Caress's *Hank Williams: Country Music's Tragic King*. In his second edition of *From Life to Legend*, Rivers corrected a few errors and added a discography of the recordings made by the Drifting Cowboys after their reorganization in 1977.

The best early discography, however, came from Bob Pinson of The Country Music Foundation Library and Media Center in Nashville. It appeared at the end of the second edition of Roger M. Williams's *Sing a Sad Song*. Pinson worked with individual songs, identifying the place and date of the recording of each as well as the records on which a song appeared. Thus, we might learn that "Calling You" was recorded in Nashville on 11 December 1946 and that the song appeared on Sterling 201, MGM 11628, MGM K11628, MGM X4220, MGM X1648, MGM E243, MGM E3331,

MGM 3E2, and MGM SE4576. Pinson also gives composer credits for most songs. His information is plentiful and meticulous, providing for the careful reader a fine history of the recording career of Hank Williams. I should note that Pinson and Charles K. Wolfe did the notes for the 1981 Time/Life Country and Western Classics issue (TLCW-01). These notes, the biographical sketch by Roger Williams, and the thirty-nine carefully selected songs on the three LPs serve as a landmark in the serious and scholarly treatment of Hank Williams. The discography for my book, *Hank Williams: A Bio-bibliography*, is largely based on Pinson's work. I tried to give it a format that would reveal quickly the magnitude of Hank's songwriting and recording career. Pinson, I understand, is at work now on a chronological discography; my guess is that work will eventually be the standard.

Meanwhile, Colin Escott has led us into the compact-disc era. His *Hank Williams: The Biography* concludes with a discography that emphasizes the compact-disc productions. Perhaps more important, though, is Escott's work in making the music available on compact disc. He compiled and produced the 1990 issue "Hank Williams: The Original Singles Collection" (Polydor 847 194 4, Polygram 847 194 2). The set covers all of the singles released during Hank's lifetime and comes with Escott's introduction to the biography and discographical entries on each of the eighty-four songs.

In 1998, on what should have been Hank's seventy-fifth birthday, Escott (with Kira Florita and The Country Music Foundation) followed with the monumental ten-compact-disc collection "The Complete Hank Williams" (Mercury 314 536 077 2). The first thing out of this attractive package is a fine booklet, 118 pages of information on Hank and his music, the commentary generously supported by numerous photographs, many of them published there for the first time. Among many other things, we get to see several rare family pictures, the handwritten manuscripts of "I Saw the Light" and "Cold, Cold Heart," and a rather moving letter to Hank from Fred Rose about drinking too much.

The booklet is introduced by Daniel Cooper's concise and well-written biographical essay "No More Darkness, No More Night," followed by Escott's extensive notes on the music (with discographical information by Bob Pinson). These are more than notes. They include good information on the studios, the recording formats, and the workings of the record charts. The notes also include much biographical detail as Escott works through Hank's recording and performing career. Additionally, there is a chart history (1947–1989) that reminds us graphically of Hank's popularity, as does the list of achievements and awards. Bob Pinson's "14 Days on the Road: Hank's Datebook from March 23 to April 7, 1951" is nicely presented. The booklet ends with Escott's brief essay "The Death of Hank Williams" and a chronology.

Obviously, though, people buy the set for the music. The 225 tracks include the Sterling and MGM studio recordings plus 53 less available pieces. Many of the latter were taken from Montgomery demos and radio performances; the Shreveport radio performances; Nashville demos; and a series of radio, television, and concert performances. Very notably, Escott includes Hank's spoken apology for a missed performance. He does not include the complete AFRS transcriptions or all of the songs performed on the "Health and Happiness" shows; in some cases Escott found better productions of particular songs elsewhere. But he does include five numbers that were recorded on only those shows. For example, Escott's set includes Hank's AFRS performance of "Let the Spirit Descend," the only commercial issue of that song.

The set has been well received, but the claim of "complete" has led to some objections. Thomas Wilmeth's very clear summary of Hank's recording career, in a 1999 essay for *The Papers of the Biographical Society of America,* lays these out concisely.[1] Wilmeth's most aggressive complaint is that the Escott set claims "Hank's debut on the Grand Ole Opry." That 11 June 1949 moment was not recorded, and Escott replaces it with the 18 June 1949 Opry performance of "Lovesick Blues." Wilmeth says that, in this matter, the set "appears to be purposefully misleading" (403). Wilmeth goes on to note the performance of "I Can't Help It" that Hank did with Anita Carter on *The Kate Smith Family Hour;* Wilmeth believes that

Hank's "Cold, Cold Heart" that night is a cut at least as important as Escott's choice. For "a total aural portrait," Wilmeth would like to hear a few takes of Audrey with Hank "as a solo backing guitarist" (404). He also notes the many complications, some of them legal, involved with takes from the "Mother's Best" and the "Duck Head" shows that Hank did for WSM in Nashville. As Wilmeth puts it, "the fact that these various radio performances are not included in the COMPLETE set, or anywhere else, cannot be helped. However, the fact that essayist Colin Escott does not acknowledge their existence in the notes to this 1998 collection is troubling, since it begs the question about what other elements of the Williams canon are purposefully being ignored" (405).

To be fair to both parties, Wilmeth, a convincing scholar, has plenty of praise for Escott, both as producer and as biographer. I suggest that the Escott set is as close as we have gotten to Hank Williams and, taken with Wilmeth's strong essay, it becomes a full representation of the work of Hank Williams and of the many complications involved in making that work available.

Escott (with Kira Florita) made an additional contribution to the compact-disc era with 1999 issue, "Hank Williams Live at the Grand Ole Opry" (Mercury 314 546 466 2). The two-volume set reproduces the AFRS recordings of the Opry for troops overseas. This issue comes with an introduction by Pulitzer Prize–winning author Rick Bragg, who reminisces about the presence of Hank's music in his childhood. The first compact disc includes twenty-one of Hank's performances: Nineteen of them are from the AFRS discs, and the other two are previously unissued versions of "Window Shopping" and "Long Gone Lonesome Blues" that were taken from Carl Smith's "Fortune Feeds" segment of the Opry. Escott notes that these two songs were performed on 5 July 1952, about a month before Jim Denny would fire Hank Williams.

Disc 2, identified as a "bonus disc," is the complete AFRS show of 18 February 1950. Its takes include two by Hank and eight by such others as Red Foley, Minnie Pearl, Jamup and Honey, Claude Sharpe and the Old

Hickory Singers, and Wally Fowler and the Oak Ridge Quartet. In his liner notes, Escott explains that his intention was to let us hear Hank as "part of a fast-paced music and variety revue," the way "his original listeners experienced him."

Most of Hank's music remains in print and is easy enough to find. The two WSFA songbooks present the only difficulty: They are rare, and unfortunately the books include only the words of the songs because Hank hoped his fans would tune in to pick up the melodies from his radio shows. The first one, *Songs of Hank Williams, "The Drifting Cowboy,"* came out in about 1945. The uncopyrighted book sold for 35¢ and included the words of ten songs. The second book, *Hank Williams and His Drifting Cowboys, Stars of WSFA, Deluxe Song Book,* came out in 1946 and is a little fancier than its predecessor. It includes the words of thirty songs along with prefaces by Hank and WSFA Program Director Caldwell Stewart. The book is uncopyrighted. These two collections are important because they show us the work Hank had done before he met Fred Rose and demonstrate the basic characteristics that would always be a part of Hank's work—the simplicity, sincerity, and directness that he never gave up. It is unfortunate that the books are so hard to come by. I found photocopies of them in The Country Music Foundation Library and Media Center in Nashville and a few random pages from them in the Alabama Department of Archives and History in Montgomery.

The sheet music for Hank's better known songs is available in several forms. Fred Rose Music published three souvenir songbooks: *Hank Williams' Country Music Folio, Hank Williams' Country Hit Parade,* and *Hank Williams' Favorite Songs.* Each includes a short introduction by Rose, several photographs, and twenty songs. We should keep in mind, however, that the sixty songs covered by the series come to fewer than half of Hank's complete work. Hal Leonard Publishing's *The Best of Hank Williams* collects thirty songs, and Acuff-Rose's *The Songs of Hank Williams* includes fifty-five numbers, a brief essay by Melvin Shestack, and a discography with twenty-two entries. The music from the film of Hank's life, which starred

George Hamilton, is available in *Songs from Your Cheatin' Heart*. In addition to the music, the book has a brief introduction by Sam Katzman, producer of the MGM picture, and includes a series of stills from the film. Probably the best source of Hank's music is *Hank Williams: The Complete Works: A 128 Song Legacy of His Music*. Interesting here are composer credits that clearly indicate the various collaborations. For those who wish to take Hank just as poet, Don Cusic has edited a nice little book, *Hank Williams: The Complete Lyrics*.

Other than the songs, Hank left little primary material for biographers. He kept no journals and wrote no autobiography. His few letters are little more than notes. He did many interviews, but, like the one I cited in chapter 1, these were mainly promotional items that Hank did with disc jockeys as he pulled in and out of towns. Those times were short—in his prime, Hank was doing 200 one-nighters a year—and there was no journalist traveling with him to record intimate details of life on the road. Besides, Hank's drinking did not always leave him in the best shape for chitchat.

Allen Rankin tried to keep up with Hank around Montgomery, but he got little of substance. In a discussion about writing a song, Hank disingenuously told Rankin that "if it takes any longer than 15 minutes I know the idea is no good and throw it away."[2] When Rankin asked him about a Luke the Drifter number, Hank replied: "Don't know why I happened to of wrote that thing. Except somebody that's fell, he's the same man, ain't he, as before he fell? Got the same blood in his veins, ain't he? So how can he be such a nice guy when he's got nothin'? Can you tell me?"[3]

Ray Jenkins, another Alabama journalist, had less luck when he tried to interview Hank in Columbus, Georgia during one of the Hadacol Caravan tours. The newsman told Roger Williams: "I couldn't figure out if he was drunk or what, but he didn't say much, and I couldn't make sense out of what he did say. I didn't even write a story about him."[4] Hank did not go too deep even when he was coherent. In a *Country Song Roundup* interview, he revealed that his favorite record was "Cold, Cold Heart," his favorite food was chicken, his favorite color was blue, his favorite entertainers were Johnny Ray and Moon Mullican, and he did have a record collection.[5] Jerry Rivers reports that California disc jockey Cottonseed Clark asked Hank why his songs were so sad. Hank replied: "Well, Cottonseed, I guess I always have been a sadist."[6] Hank seemed to be a little more garrulous in a Melvin Shestack interview done near Rochester, New York, in 1948. Shestack says he was doing the piece for his high school newspaper, but the faculty adviser refused to print it. He tells of meeting Hank and of having hot dogs and soft drinks with him. The interview, often reprinted, is atypical, and those who know the travels well are convinced that Hank was not in New York at the time.[7]

Hank said so little that many of the interviews turn out to be articles with a sprinkling of quotes from him. Ralph Gleason's June 1952 interview is like that. Gleason was working for the *San Francisco Chronicle* when he went out to the Leamington Hotel in Oakland to talk to the singer. When Gleason went into the hotel room, Hank was in the lavatory. When he came out, according to Gleason, he "went over to the top of the bureau, swept off a handful of pills and deftly dropped them, one at a time, with short expert slugs from the glass." They went down to the coffee shop for breakfast, where Hank recalled singing at Mount Olive Church, following Tee Tot, and his first recording session. He called his music "folk music" and explained that "the tunes are simple and easy to remember and the singers, they're sincere about them." Hank cited Johnny Ray and then claimed that Roy Acuff is "the biggest singer this music ever knew." Gleason intended to follow up on the promising interview, but says that "at the intermission, it was impossible to talk to him. He was a little stoned and he didn't seem to remember our conversation earlier in the day and the party was beginning to get a little rough. They were whiskey drinkers and so I gave them room, looked around a while and then went on back out."[8] This squeamishness, remarkable in a journalist who would later write for *Rolling Stone*, left Gleason without much of an interview, so he turned out an essay about the difficulty of talking to Hank Williams.

Rufus Jarman was a little harder to frighten, and he got a few good comments for a *Nation's Business* article on the urbanization of country music. His interview took place not long before Hank died, and it includes the most often quoted statements by the star. Hank emphasized the sincerity of the good country singer and said that "when a hillbilly sings a crazy song, he feels crazy. When he sings, 'I Laid My Mother Away,' he sees her a-laying right there in the coffin." The reason for the sincerity is that the hillbilly singer was brought up in tough circumstances; he knew about life, about hard work. In Hank's words, "you got to have smelt a lot of mule manure before you can sing like a hillbilly. The people who had been raised something like the way the hillbilly has knows what he is singing about and appreciates it." His songs, Hank added, were for the common people, American or otherwise. And he argued that the music revealed quite a bit about American life.[9] These statements are no profundities, but they are about as much as could be squeezed out of Hank Williams.

That Hank did so little to identify himself or to analyze his music has two major effects, I think. One is that he thereby maintained his authenticity. On and off stage, Hank Williams was the plain country boy from somewhere down in Alabama. Second, Hank's silence opened the door to the mythology. Close kin like Lillie and Audrey were eager to fill in the chasms with their own fanciful versions of the biography. Other relatives followed suit, and the Opry inner circle of the day did not know just what to say because Hank's behavior usually clashed with the wholesome image they had worked hard to cultivate. Unravelling it all has become the work of those of us eager to establish the real biography, and we are many.

Colin Escott joined us most recently. His book, *Hank Williams: The Biography*, is important in filling in details of Hank's recording career. Escott, a Canadian music critic well known for his *Good Rockin' Tonight: Sun Records and the Birth of Rock and Roll* and for his production of the compact-disc set *The Complete Hank Williams*, is thorough in his purpose of placing Hank Williams "in the context of the music industry of his day, not ours, and to show how the industry grew around him during the years that he lived" (xi). And he gives us plenty of details about recording sessions, bands, sidemen, and itineraries. Escott exercises his breadth well in his brave and honest speculations about what might have happened to Hank had he lived on through the 1950s and into the 1960s. Elvis was coming on strong in the early 1950s, and Escott's guess is that rock might have overwhelmed the hard country music that identified Hank.

I admire the fullness of this book, but I have two problems with it. First, although Escott lists numerous sources, he does not tie them to particular information. That is, we find plenty of detail, but we do not always learn where it came from, so using the book for research is difficult. My guess is that George Merritt and William MacEwen, two men who know Hank and his career as well as anyone, helped a great deal here with oral accounts. They receive credit on the title page.

The second problem I have is that the tone of the book often seems flip. Escott opens like this: "There is no business so callous or so quickly forgetful as the music business. This week's Best Bet is next week's unreturned phone call. Even the Singing Nun committed suicide" (ix). It continues, "Dead Hank became like Dead Elvis, a fly-paper that attracted myth and misinformation" (x). Hank and Audrey become "young star-crossed lovers, the bubba Rhett and Scarlett" (29). Then Hank becomes "a falling star hanging by a thread" (236). A late chapter is casually titled "The Death of Leapy the Leopard," and the last chapter, a really good piece of writing, is labeled with the bad pun, "Wuthering Depths." We should have not have been surprised, though, because near the beginning of the book Escott says "Death is a sound career move if it can be timed right, and Hank Williams's triumph was to avoid growing old disgracefully" (ix). Hank's early death certainly added to the drama of the story, and maybe it saved Hank some personal and professional agony. But the triumph is the music, which has survived well the many twists and turns of the industry.

Escott's work identifies one of the problems of biographies in popular culture: More than one writer has been self-conscious about applying serious scholarship to figures who, to mainstream culture, might seem marginal. More than one has been uneasy about applying footnotes to people like

Hank Williams. Chet Flippo, well known for his work at *Rolling Stone,*
gives us another version of that problem in *Your Cheatin' Heart: A Biogra-*
phy of Hank Williams. Flippo did extensive research into Hank's life. He
ransacked the usual sources; he researched Toby Marshall, studied Hank's
medical record and autopsy report, investigated the relationship between
Hank and Paul Gilley "who sold Hank some of his best-loved songs" (130),
and went through a collection of Audrey's private papers.

But Flippo resisted the idea of the critical biography that he was so
well qualified to write. Instead, in an attempt to give the life "immediacy
and fire" (7), he takes a tactic that nearly becomes fiction, especially as he
imagines a large amount of dialogue for the characters. The facts are plentiful, but the book, in large part, takes liberties with them as Flippo goes
after what he took to be the real Hank Williams. The attempt, I think, was to
give *Your Cheatin' Heart* an especially broad audience. Like much of Nashville's music, the book is designed to be a crossover hit—one that country
music fans would not miss, one that those who know little about country
music could enjoy. Many of Hank's fans will be put off by the laid-bare version of the man Flippo presents. Those pursuing history are going to be
frustrated because Flippo's kind of writing does not separate fact from in-
terpretation. But no one is going to be denied a good read in this volume.
Moreover, Flippo's view of the singer and composer as a hard, depressed,
and largely antisocial character is a necessary slant in the search for Hank
Williams.

The appeal that Flippo seems to want calls less for the ordinary and
more for the shocking, and sometimes he overdraws his characters and sit-
uations. For example, we see Lillie, at 225 pounds, snatching the 5-pound infant Hank from her own womb, holding him up like a rabbit to be chopped
behind the ears while a tobacco road Lon is drunk on the front porch. Lon
was well-versed in his wife's right-cross. Young Hank was to learn quickly
from his dad and, according to Flippo, spent time hiding in the graveyard. If
this is fiction, it is heavy-handed; if it is fact, it could have been put more
subtly. The point, though, is good enough; these broadly drawn opening

scenes and characters show us the basis of Hank's weakness, the ease with which women would always dominate him and the deceptive solace he would find in a jug. Flippo's research on the alcoholism reveals many of Hank's stays in sanitariums, beginning with the one in Prattville, Alabama in 1945; his speculation about Hank growing up under Lillie's thumb is that it explains why Hank had so much difficulty forming real friendships with men.

Flippo identifies the early spinal problem, the "spina bifida occulta of the first sacral segment of the lower spine" (153), and his medical research here is convincing. He gives an interesting version of Audrey, a passionate country girl who started sleeping with Hank long before she was divorced from her first husband. Her devious use of sex to get her way is certainly a major thread in Flippo's view of the marriage. Like Lillie, Audrey takes plenty of shots from Flippo, who sees her infidelity as one of Hank's major problems. He is, moreover, the first to identify in print Audrey's divorcing of Hank on 26 May 1948, exactly a year before the birth of Hank Jr. He notes, of course, that the divorce was amended *nunc pro tunc* on 9 August 1949.

Another issue that Flippo takes up is the amount of collaboration involved in Hank's songwriting. We may like the image of Hank as spontaneous composer, as one whose sensitivity overflowed into fine songs. Evidently, Hank had as much of that gift as anyone; but at the same time, many writers, among them Ed Linn and Roger Williams, have discussed the help he got from Fred Rose and Vic McAlpin. Without giving us too much evidence, Flippo dwells on this issue, implying that Hank may have received more help than we thought and arguing that Paul Gilley, a Moorehead State College basketball player, wrote versions of "I'm So Lonesome I Could Cry" and "Cold, Cold Heart." This view shows the easy commerce between young songwriters and established stars. But I wish that Flippo provided more hard facts and less the air of expose.

A few other points need mentioning. Flippo has an interesting view of Hank's relationship with his audiences. Almost everyone agrees that Hank was an expert at handling them; but late in his career and deep into his alcoholism, he could be contemptuous of his crowds and difficult on stage. Flippo believes the alcohol brought out a truly antisocial streak that probably had its origin in Hank's street peddling and shoeshining. He was, Flippo implies, willing to accept the money and praise of shoeshine customers, but he was resentful of those who would put him through his paces in such a way. I am not sure that the parallel between shining shoes and performing for adoring throngs holds up, but perhaps it portrays accurately a facet of Hank's personality—or maybe it just reminds us of the surliness that alcohol can bring on.

Flippo goes into some detail with regard to Hank's sex life, with Audrey and Billie Jean and a few others, including at least one fifteen-year-old. Once again, verification would be interesting, although documenting the deeds of the night has never been easy. Another point that gets attention concerns Hank's death, which has been shrouded in the mystery of what and how much Hank was taking and drinking at the time. Flippo gives this a turn by speculating that Hank had been in a barroom fight shortly before his death and that his injuries may have contributed to his end. But again, we have only speculation. Flippo's other addition here is that last song, the love note, perhaps to Audrey, that Hank supposedly clutched as he died. As I have suggested already, we should be cautious about accepting this story as fact.

Roger Williams, one of the best-known Williams scholars, gives us a more traditional biography, and serious students of the star are much indebted to him. Doubleday published his *Sing a Sad Song: The Life of Hank Williams* in 1970; Ballantine Books put out a paperback edition of it in 1973; and the University of Illinois Press published the second edition of the volume as part of its Music in American Life series in 1981. This second edition is the most accessible, and it is the most valuable of the three because it includes the fine discography by Bob Pinson of The Country Music Foundation Library and Media Center. Unfortunately, the book does not include the photographs that are part of the paperback. More unfortunately, the book was printed from the plates of the 1970 edition, so Roger Williams's very brief afterword and Pinson's discography are the only updates.

This biography's particular strength is its treatment of Hank's youth. The coverage is extensive, the mythology is kept in its place, and the credibility is strong because of the author's numerous interviews with Hank's family and acquaintances. These interviews are particularly valuable because the number of family and friends is diminishing fast. Another strength, certain to appeal to country fans in general and Hank Williams fans in particular, is the calm and nonsensational perspective. Hank Williams here is a wild enough character, but he is not quite so bizarre as Chet Flippo imagined.

As this book gives the basic facts of the biography, it also shows some of the problems of dealing with Hank Williams. Roger Williams misses the date of the marriage of Lillie and Lon; he assigns the 1916 wedding to 1918, probably because Lillie herself, maybe confused by her several weddings, gave 1918 as the year. In working out the source of Hank's back problem without early medical records, Williams could make only the bad guess that the child fell off ice skates. His discussions of Alabama lynchings and the slayings of civil rights workers by way of backdrop seem extraneous as do some of the digressions on whiskey stills, Southern politics, and the origins of musical instruments.

In spite of my complaints, *Sing a Sad Song* will continue to be a major part of Hank Williams scholarship. It is, as I have said, careful and sensibly calm. I would recommend that readers, as they finish the book, turn to Roger Williams's subsequent essays on Hank. One is in the 1975 volume *Stars of Country Music: Uncle Dave Macon to Johnny Rodriguez*, which was edited by Bill C. Malone and Judith McCulloh. The other is in the 1981 booklet that comes with the Time/Life Country and Western Classics issue that I mentioned above. Both of these essays reflect the work of a writer who has done very careful research and had time to think about it and to temper it with more recent work.

Another book generally counted important is *Hank Williams: Country Music's Tragic King* by Jay Caress, a country disc jockey, singer, editor, and converted Christian from Illinois. For the most part, Caress works with materials presented by Roger Williams, extrapolating them with some odd ideas and some purple prose. For example, Hank gets compared to King Saul, King Lear, and Van Gogh, all in one paragraph. Hank's marriage to Audrey, in the hands of Caress, comes to be like that of Lincoln to Mary Todd. Another discussion points out that "Every great and popular artist has been an unknown at one point" (61). A discussion of "the art of pain" suggests that "It's almost as if one night Edgar Allan Poe had delivered by cosmic mail his invisible mantle of pain's dark hidden wisdom to some iron bridge down on some back-country creek between Montgomery and Shreveport" (91). Later we find that audiences were "slapped into Silly Putty by Hank Williams" (122). Hank, I am afraid, was born too early for Silly Putty.

Caress writes better prose when he is sure of his subject. He is reasonable on Hank's death and the circumstances surrounding it. He is helpful, too, with a concluding summary of what has happened to the story's major characters since Hank's death. But otherwise, the book is not up to the subject. Some confused facts and the acceptance of some of the myth as fact spoil its credibility. The conclusion, which sees Hank heading for his eternal reward, is almost bizarre. All of us wish heaven for Hank Williams; few though have visualized it as clearly as Jay Caress, who has God watching Hank "take his solitary ride into eternity." Caress goes on to describe the view of the world from various heights as Hank travels upward. Finally, the departed hero has "this sense of, of glory... There was a magnetic presence, an energizing aliveness to the space he floated in, yet the perfection he felt was still nothing he could see—it merely affected the way he saw everything else" (231).

Jerry Rivers's *Hank Williams: From Life to Legend* adds another dimension to the materials on Hank. Rivers, Hank's fiddler from 1949 to 1952, deals less with scholarly detail and much more with the impressions and anecdotes appropriate for a memoir. This reminiscence sticks mostly to the period during which Rivers knew Hank and is thus a useful resource for The Grand Ole Opry part of the biography; the book is particularly good on the Hadacol Caravan tour. The discography, as I have noted, has been superseded, but the collection of photos of Hank's funeral is the best in print.

Horace Logan, a Shreveport radio producer much involved in developing the Louisiana Hayride, tells us about that part of Hank's life in *Elvis, Hank, and Me: Making Musical History on the Louisiana Hayride*. Logan is a little too intent on being king maker here, but his well-embroidered anecdotes are good fun. He says that he wanted Hank on the Hayride the minute he heard his tapes, but was fearful of the drinking. He contacted Hank, and they made this deal: If the promising young star could stay sober for six months, Logan would put him on the show. Hank kept his word, at least according to Logan, and in July of 1948, he, Audrey, and Lycrecia showed up in Shreveport in an old Chrysler with a mattress and box spring tied on top. Hank made his famous 7 August 1948 debut and continued with the Hayride, at $24 per performance, for nearly a year before heading to the Opry. That success story, of course, turned tragic when Hank, dismissed from the Opry in 1952, returned to the Hayride a broken man, well received by Logan nonetheless.

Logan adds some details about Hank's descent and some comments about Billie Jean, who he knew fairly well. He is convinced that Hank married her so fast because he feared Lillie would intervene. Logan is also convinced that Hank, because he signed a three-year contract that would have kept him on the Hayride well into 1955 (at $200 per Saturday night), had no real plan to return to Nashville and Audrey. Like Chet Flippo, Logan speculates that Hank's death may have involved some violence. All in all, these memories and speculations come from sizeable distance and do not have as much convincing immediacy as those by Jerry Rivers.

Another reminiscence of value, but perhaps for the wrong reasons, is Lillie Williams's *Our Hank Williams: "The Drifting Cowboy."* Lillie, who told her story to Montgomery journalist Allen Rankin, is often wrong about details and is generally self-serving. Her comment that Hank was only five when Lon left belongs more to the wronged wife than to history. She is much further off in her claim to have left Hank in Mobile for only three weeks instead of the nearly two years indicated by the records of the Alabama Shipbuilding and Drydock Company. And, as I said earlier, she is wrong to call Hank "a sort of preacher at heart." Apparently Lillie misunderstood her son's back problem completely. She describes it this way: "With all of his traveling he had developed a spinal injury. He had to have an operation. Some people thought that the way Hank trembled and 'suffered' over a song was part of his act but his friends knew that the 'act' was real. He was suffering continuously." Lillie has her most dependable moment as she describes the relationship of Hank and Audrey: "They say the course of true love never runs smoothly. Certainly it didn't in this case."

The value of the little book, which sold for $1 through the mails, is that it identifies the source of some of the myth while revealing a good share of the mother's personality. Lillie is the one who tells the tale of Hank's writing "Mansion on the Hill" by way of proving his songwriting ability to Fred Rose. Whereas history has Hank and Audrey calling on Fred, Lillie has Fred hearing "Move It on Over" and calling Hank in for a contract. Lillie was always eager to keep Audrey's part minimal and to give herself a major role in practically everything her son did. *Our Hank Williams*, I think, is really Lillie's Hank Williams.

Each of the three children involved has written a book, the first being Hank Jr.'s *Living Proof*. This quick autobiography focuses on the nearly fatal 1975 mountain-climbing accident that may have brought Jr. to his senses. He tells us much about life in the shadow of Hank Williams, but, because he was only three when his father died, he does not cut very deeply into that shadow. Hank Jr. reminds us that Audrey "just plain couldn't sing" (77), and he talks about his struggle with his mother, who wanted him to imitate directly his father while he was more interested in the rock that was sweeping over the music scene of his youth, a conflict that eventually led him in the direction of Waylon Jennings and the outlaw movement. His great moment came in a 1976 concert in Delaware when, he says dramatically, "I played my music. Not Daddy's music. Not Mother's music. But my own music" (190). The book, not surprisingly, is a fan item on behalf of Hank Jr. and not a lot of help in the research of his father.

Lycrecia, Audrey's child by Erskine Guy, does a better job in *Still in Love with You: The Story of Hank and Audrey Williams.* She can get sentimental about Hank and Audrey. Like Hank Jr., she is sure the pair would have reconciled had Hank lived, and her attempt to place the domestic problems into the context of scientific studies of alcoholism does not get very far. But Lycrecia is a pretty tough storyteller much of the time. She confirms a number of the rumors and stories about the Williams's personal life, in particular about Audrey and Lillie physically fighting, about Hank firing a shot at Audrey. Lycrecia seems clear to me when she says "Mother was not what you call a doting parent. She was good to us and showed us love, but she wasn't the kind that coddled you a lot. Daddy did a lot more coddling. Mother took a lot of time with Hank, Jr., but she wasn't the type to be tied to the house because of the children" (49–50). She also gives us long and helpful quotes from friends of the Williams family and from Audrey's unpublished memoir, most of these available nowhere else as far as I know. Lycrecia is also a good source on Audrey's life after Hank's death, that spiral of wheeling and dealing, of booze and drugs, that ended in her mother's pathetic death in 1975. I admire the way Lycrecia maintains the context of the lives of her parents as she tells her own story.

The best of the three books is *Ain't Nothin' as Sweet as My Baby: The Story of Hank Williams' Lost Daughter* by Jett Williams, Hank's illegitimate daughter by Bobbie Jett. I find the book dependable and have used it extensively in my summary of Jett's life at the end of chapter 1. I appreciate especially the chronology and the quotes from, and references to, pertinent legal documents. Jett, of course, cannot give us first-hand details about her father, but she is really good at mixing her own powerful story with Hank's biography, never letting one overwhelm the other.

A few other books deserve mention. Robert K. Krishef's *Hank Williams* is a brief biography written for children. The book is direct and well written, accessible without being condescending. Notably, Krishef does not avoid Hank's drinking or his marriage to Billie Jean, two items that Lillie steers around carefully in her book.

Thurston Moore's *Hank Williams, the Legend* is a collection of articles that range from good scholarship to maudlin fan rag stuff. For example, Bill C. Malone's fine introduction, "Hank Williams: Voice of Tradition in a Period of Change," is followed by Irene Williams Smith's Ouija-board approach, "My Treasured Life with a Beloved Brother." The volume reprints John Stephen Doherty's "Hank Williams Won't Die," an article better than its title, especially in its treatment of Hank's adult life and his involvements with women. A good collection of liner notes, written by everyone from Paul Ackerman to Nat Hentoff, is reproduced along with many sentimental reminiscences, a recipe for crawfish pie, a discography, an interview, and a useful assortment of news clippings.

Three booklets add some details, especially about Hank's boyhood. The most recent is *Hank as We Knew Him*, published by the Three Arts Club of Georgiana and Chapman, Alabama, in 1982. It lists no author but is copyrighted in the name of Sherry Bowers. The twenty-four pages focus on Hank's local reputation and include some good photos of the boyhood haunts along with some clippings from the *Butler County News*. Mr. and Mrs. Burton Odom prepared a similar booklet, *The Hank Williams Story*, published by the Butler County Historical Association in 1974. Largely dependent on Roger Williams, this pamphlet gathers the essentials of Hank's life and adds a few new comments by acquaintances. Harry E. Rockwell's *Beneath the Applause*, published privately by Rockwell in 1973, is the story of a fan's pilgrimage through Hank's world. Its particular interests are an interview with Lon Williams and some good details gathered from those in Oak Hill, West Virginia who were associated with Hank's death.

Several books help in establishing Hank's context. Paul Hemphill's *The Nashville Sound: Bright Lights and Country Music* gives us a good taste of Nashville's atmosphere and finds Hank a rounder who did much to give the wholesome city a more worldly tint. Michael Bane's *White Boy*

Singin' the Blues: The Black Roots of White Rock has Hank caught between the heavy influences of blues and the primarily white world of country music. Peter Guralnick's *Lost Highway: Journeys and Arrivals of American Musicians* is a great read that places Hank into the world of the blues and honky-tonk. Nick Tosches, always readable and usually outrageous, is good on Hank's influences on rock in *Country: The Biggest Music in America.*

The most scholarly books on the Nashville music scene are by John W. Rumble and Bill C. Malone. Rumble's dissertation, "Fred Rose and the Development of the Nashville Music Industry, 1942–1954" explains very clearly the intricacies of music publishing, and it includes many details of Hank's relationship with Acuff-Rose. Rumble notes that Hank often "depended on Rose to complete compositions he [Hank] had begun" (126) and that the association with Hank "largely accounted for Rose's recognition and commercial prosperity" (116). Malone's book, *Country Music U.S.A.: A Fifty-Year History,* published for the American Folklore Society's Memoir series, is a thorough work that finds that "Williams was the symbol of country music's postwar upsurge ... his sudden death in 1953 signified the ending of the boom period" (232). More recently, Malone has published *Singing Cowboys and Musical Mountaineers: Southern Culture and the Roots of Country Music.* The book, based on lectures given by Malone for Mercer University's Lamar Series, is a very rich and well-informed commentary on country music in general and includes reference to Hank in a discussion of country singers who cultivated a western image. This is the book I would recommend to those who want to understand what country music and country music scholarship are all about.

Dealing with the articles in newspapers and magazines is nearly impossible. Much of that material is of the "fan" variety and is not much help to researchers. Most of the material that is substantially historical has been absorbed by the many books on Hank. Those who want to sample this material should see the clippings files at The Country Music Foundation Library and Media Center in Nashville and at the Department of Archives and History in Montgomery. Most major newspapers have files on Hank. I list a number of the more important articles in the bibliography, but call particular attention to David Halberstam's clean summary of Hank's life and unsentimental evaluation of his music in *Look* (13 July 1971); David Mankelow's "Legend" (*Country*, April 1973), which is a good twenty-years-after appraisal of Hank and his influences; and Nick Tosches's comments on the music in the special Hank Williams issue of *Country Music* (March 1975).

The movies have not done very well by Hank. The little drama of MGM's *Your Cheatin' Heart* pales beside the reality. Also, the idea that George Hamilton could play Hank Williams convincingly is far-fetched— Roger Williams offers amusing praise when, in *Sing a Sad Song*, he says that Hamilton was a better choice to play Hank than Sammy Davis Jr. (241). And Susan Oliver's Audrey makes us think we are watching *Tammy Goes to Nashville*. The screenplay is no stronger than the cast. Hank sings "Jesus Loves Me" as Tee Tot dies in his arms. Then he deserts a medicine show to join Audrey's band, the Drifting Cowboys. Hank plays out his part as the mischievous drunk, falling off a horse while celebrating the birth of Hank Jr., singing with orchestral backup music, and finally drying out only to pass away in the back seat of his car. Notably absent from the film are Hank's divorce from Audrey and his marriage to Billie Jean. That Audrey was MGM's technical adviser may explain the oversights.

I understand that Paul Schrader, who wrote *American Gigolo, Taxi Driver,* and *Raging Bull,* prepared a script for a really tough version of Hank's life, but the film has never been made. I understand, too, that the Jett Williams story is to be made into a movie. In a recent e-mail, Keith Adkinson, Jett's husband and manager, told me that "Jett's movie is still in the works for CBS airing with de Passe Entertainment, but nothing's done til it's done." So, for the moment, the only real evidence of Hank in Hollywood is in the songs that dominate the sound track of *The Last Picture Show.*

The television special "A Tribute to Hank Williams: The Man and His Music," which aired in Nashville on 12 April 1980, includes a respectable biography. Jim Owen, known for his one-man Hank Williams performance, is good enough as Hank. Although Laney Smallwood does not look much like Audrey, she plays the part well. The script, by Nashville's Billy and Pat Galvin, is far more realistic than that of the MGM movie. Audrey is not the ever-loving wife this time out; she is cruel enough to leave an ailing Hank at home in bed while she goes out on the town, and Hank is mean enough to take a few shots at her for her trouble. The television film, however, is really just a series of clips cut into basic entertainment supplied by a series of distinguished singers. Hosted by Hank Jr., the special features Brenda Lee, Faron Young, Kris Kristofferson, Johnny Cash, Waylon Jennings, Teresa Brewer, and Roy Acuff. It is much more a progression of highlights than a complete document, and it gets sentimental as it approaches the death scene. But the program does mark an advance by including the harder side of Hank.

Alabama writer Babs Deal was the first to try a novel based on Hank's life. *High Lonesome World: The Death and Life of a Country Singer* claims no historical reference but is about Hank in almost every detail. It includes familiar characters: Wade Coley is a pale Hank who dies on his way to an engagement in Memphis; Audrey becomes Lorene, the divorcee who wants to be the widow; Billie Jean is Kitty, the new wife; Lillie is Maud, the distressed mother; Luke the Drifter turns up as The Wanderer; and Tee Tot is the shuffling and talented Linc Smith. Although received reasonably well thirty years ago, *High Lonesome World* seems very dated now, especially in its two-dimensional picture of Hank and country music.

Roy Campbell's *Hustler* story "Little Skeeter's Gotta Learn" is about a girl named Cathy who is seduced on the day of Hank's death. She is so pleased with herself and so anxious for more that she leaves home, pretending that she is going to Hank's funeral. Actually, she is off to be a hooker. Skeeter, her young admirer, learns of how Cathy has abused the memory of Hank, beats her senseless, and then starts his own pilgrimage to Hank's grave. This is not high art, but Campbell may have the right idea in letting Hank be more a presence than a character here.

Kinky Friedman did something similar in *A Case of Lone Star*. In this funny and tough-talking novel, Kinky is his own hero, at times the leader of a country band, "The Texas Jewboys," at times a seedy New York private eye. He is just the guy to figure out the mystery at hand. A number of country musicians have been murdered, and all of the clues come from songs by Hank Williams. Amusingly, Chet Flippo, one of Hank's real-life biographers, turns up as a suspect. In another funny murder mystery, *Roadkill*, Kinky is on the road with Willie Nelson—and the spirit of Hank Williams.

In their failures and successes, these four works of fiction and the films I have mentioned make an important point when taken together: The life of Hank Williams was so stunning in and of itself that dramatizing it seems unnecessary and nearly impossible. At the same time, though, the life and the music are so pervasive, such landmarks, that they serve easily as backdrops for work referring to country music, for half a century of a large segment of American life.

The major repositories of Hank Williams material reflect two approaches to the life and music. The more pop version is the Hank Williams Museum that recently opened in Montgomery's old Union Station. It features the 1952 Cadillac that Hank died in along with a number of paintings of Hank, some of them as eerie as the mysterious "H" and "W" that seem to be visible in the woodwork to close observers. The collection, still in progress, includes such items as an Audrey cowhide purse, some of Hank's King Edward cigars, one of his pistols, a fancy cowboy saddle, and a Steinway piano. I hear that the Montgomery Chamber of Commerce has discussed moving Hank's grave into the building. The museum replaces its predecessor, which operated briefly on Nashville's 16th Avenue South.

The Country Music Foundation Library and Media Center, now in its new quarters on the corner of Fifth Avenue and Demonbreun in Nashville, is more serious. Its most striking item is a continuing exhibit called "The Treasures of Hank Williams." Made up in part of memorabilia purchased from Irene Williams Smith by country performer Marty Stuart, it includes several song manuscripts (most notably those of "Your Cheatin' Heart" and "Cold, Cold Heart"), along with such personal items as stage uniforms, glasses, fishing gear, and letters to relatives and to Fred Rose. Even the most casual fan has to be taken by this moving tribute to "The Poet of the People."

The library has complete holdings of literature on country music; a record collection of well over 100,000 volumes; a large collection of films about or including country music figures; and a collection of videotapes of many country music television shows, along with a variety of home movies involving important personalities. The Hank Williams recordings and literature are there as is a print of the MGM film, *Your Cheatin' Heart.* The collection includes a kinescope of Hank on *The Kate Smith Evening Hour* in 1952, a home movie of one of Lycrecia's birthday parties, a film of the September 1954 Hank Williams Memorial Day celebration in Montgomery, and the television show "A Tribute to Hank Williams: The Man and His Music." Another valuable resource housed here is the collection of AFRS transcriptions of The Grand Ole Opry done for the military abroad.

Some of the literature on Hank is extremely rare and is probably most accessible at the foundation library. The photocopies of the two WSFA songbooks are among the holdings as well as copies of *How to Write Folk and Western Music to Sell* by Hank and Jimmy Rule, Lillie's *Our Hank Williams: "The Drifting Cowboy,"* Harry E. Rockwell's *Beneath the Applause,* Mr. and Mrs. Burton Odom's *The Hank Williams Story,* and a copy of *Hank as We Knew Him.* The library also owns a set of the ten Good Vibrations records, "Hank Williams: The Man, the Legend." These records, made primarily for radio play, blend Hank's music with a number of interviews and with a narrative of Hank's life. The interviews with the Drifting Cowboys, Faron Young, and Charles Carr (Hank's driver on the fatal trip to Canton) are particularly valuable.

The library, as I have indicated, maintains a clipping service and therefore has a good file of news stories about Hank. It owns copies of John W.

Rumble's dissertation on Fred Rose, the souvenir program for the 1954 unveiling of Hank's tomb, and the two *Hank Williams Family Photo Albums* put out by the Hank Williams Memorial Foundation. The staff includes some of the best archivists and scholars I have known, and I conclude here by thanking them for their generous help.

NOTES

Chapter 1

1. The marriage license and certificate are available from the Butler County Courthouse in Greenville, Alabama. The license was taken out on 11 November 1916 and the marriage performed on 12 November 1916. Several writers have assigned the wedding to 1918, probably because Lillie gave that date in her interviews.

2. Escott et al., *Hank Williams*, 4.

3. Flippo, *Your Cheatin' Heart*, 9.

4. Graves, *The Book of Alabama*, 58.

5. Caress, *Hank Williams*, 9; Flippo (*Your Cheatin' Heart*, 14) seems to refer to Harry E. Rockwell's *Beneath the Applause*.

6. Escott et al., *Hank Williams*, 6.

7. The Alabama Bureau of Vital Statistics searched its files covering the years 1920–1929 and found no record of the birth of Irene Williams. Irene gave me her birth date in a letter of 12 February 1984. Hank's birth certificate is available through the bureau.

8. Agee and Evans, *Let Us Now*.

9. R. M. Williams, *Sing a Sad Song*, 7–8.

10. Ibid., 41; Caress, *Hank Williams*, 34.

11. Flippo, *Your Cheatin' Heart*, 153, 208.

12. R. M. Williams, *Sing a Sad Song*, 20–23.

13. Escott et al., *Hank Williams*, 10–11.

14. Flippo, *Your Cheatin' Heart*, 34.

15. Ibid., 37.

16. R. M. Williams, *Sing a Sad Song*, 39–40.

17. L. Williams with Rankin, *Our Hank Williams.*

18. Ibid.

19. Lycrecia Williams quotes this obscure memoir extensively in her book; L. Williams with Vinicur, *Still in Love with You*, 7.

20. H. Williams Jr. with Bane, *Living Proof*, 59.

21. L. Williams with Vinicur, *Still in Love with You*, 7.

22. The divorce decree of Audrey and Erskine Guy is available at the Pike County Courthouse in Troy, Alabama.

23. L. Williams with Vinicur, *Still in Love with You*, 7.

24. The marriage license and certificate for Hank and Audrey are available in the Covington County Courthouse in Andalusia, Alabama.

25. Flippo, *Your Cheatin' Heart*, 48–49.

26. Beifuss, "Onetime," F1.

27. The full interview is printed in Koon, *Hank Williams*, 95–100.

28. Both books were published by WSFA in Montgomery; both are undated. Copies are rare. I found photo reproductions of them in The Country Music Foundation Library and Media Center in Nashville.

29. Escott et al., *Hank Williams*, 19.

30. Malone, *Country Music U.S.A.*, 187.

31. Malone and McCulloh, "Roy Acuff" in *Stars of Country Music*, 196.

32. Flippo, *Your Cheatin' Heart*, 58.

33. This letter, the other correspondence mentioned in this section, and the manuscripts of "Six More Miles" and "When God Comes and Gathers His Jewels" are available in The Country Music Foundation Library and Media Center in Nashville. Hank wrote this particular letter from 409 Washington Avenue, Montgomery. His previous address, 236 Catoma Street, had been crossed off of Audrey's letterhead.

34. Rumble, "Fred Rose," 164.

35. Logan with Sloan, *Elvis, Hank, and Me*, 24.

36. The letter is part of the collection of The Country Music Foundation Library and Media Center in Nashville.

37. The divorce decree was signed by Eugene W. Carter of the Fifteenth Judicial Courthouse in Montgomery. It is available from the Montgomery County Courthouse in Montgomery (divorce decree no. 19273).

38. The card is part of the collection of The Country Music Foundation Library and Media Center in Nashville.

39. Logan with Sloan, *Elvis, Hank, and Me*, 31.

40. R. M. Williams, *Sing a Sad Song*, 74.

41. Logan with Sloan, *Elvis, Hank, and Me*, 45, 36.

42. Hank Jr. was born at the North Louisiana Sanitarium in Shreveport. His birth certificate (no. 117 4901870) is on file with the Louisiana State Department of Health, Division of Public Statistics.

43. The telegram is part of the collection of The Country Music Foundation Library and Media Center in Nashville.

44. L. Williams with Vinicur, *Still in Love with You*, 93.

45. The decree amending the 1948 divorce is available from the Montgomery County Courthouse in Montgomery (divorce decree no. 19273).

46. Rivers, *Hank Williams*, 23.

47. The full interview is available in Koon, *Hank Williams*, 92–95.

48. The full interview is available in Koon, *Hank Williams*, 90–92.

49. The full interview is available in Koon, *Hank Williams*, 95–100.

50. R. M. Williams, *Sing a Sad Song*, 149.

51. The letter is reproduced in Rivers, *Hank Williams*, 27.

52. Flippo, *Your Cheatin' Heart*, 164.

53. Rivers, *Hank Williams*, 28.

54. Kane, *Louisiana Hayride*, 4. The best biography of Dudley LeBlanc is Clay, *Couzain Dudley LeBlanc*.

55. The full interview is available in Koon, *Hank Williams*, 95–100.

56. Rivers, *Hank Williams*, 33.

57. Flippo, *Your Cheatin' Heart*, 163.

58. R. M. Williams, *Sing a Sad Song*, 75.

59. Caress, *Hank Williams*, 100.

60. Linn, "The Short Life of Hank Williams," 89.

61. Moore, "MGM Publicist Recalls Hank Williams," in *Hank Williams*, 38. The article originally appeared in the 30 October 1965 issue of *Billboard*.

62. R. M. Williams, *Sing a Sad Song*, 176–77.

63. Ibid., 173.

64. Flippo, *Your Cheatin' Heart*, 150.

65. Ibid., 152–53.

66. Rivers, *Hank Williams*, 17.

67. L. Williams with Vinicur, *Still in Love with You,* 89.

68. Pearl with Drew, *Minnie Pearl,* 244–45.

69. The telegram is part of the collection of The Country Music Foundation Library and Media Center in Nashville.

70. The full interview is available in Koon, *Hank Williams,* 95–100.

71. Both Chet Flippo (in *Your Cheatin' Heart*) and Jay Caress (in *Hank Williams*) tell the story.

72. The marriage license and certificate are available from the Bossier Parish Courthouse, Benton, Louisiana (no. 23624).

73. Pruden, "Ol' Hank," 14.

74. The divorce decree is available from the Bossier Parish Courthouse, Benton, Louisiana (suit no. 11834). Several writers have spelled the last name "Eshlimar," but the divorce decree clearly indicates "Eshliman," as do the marriage license and certificate.

75. Flippo, *Your Cheatin' Heart,* 198.

76. Fred Bingamon, Director of Central Records for the Oklahoma Department of Corrections, gave me a copy of Marshall's rather extensive prison record.

77. Caress, *Hank Williams,* 194.

78. Rankin, "Rankin File," 29 December 1952.

79. Escott et al., *Hank Williams,* 237.

80. Morris, "Hank Williams' Death," C1.

81. R. M. Williams, *Sing a Sad Song,* 223.

82. L. Williams with Rankin, *Our Hank Williams.*

83. The best essay on Hank Williams III is Elizabeth Gilbert's "The Ghost."

Chapter 2

1. Chet Flippo prints the song in *Your Cheatin' Heart,* 206. I believe that the fragment is one of many like it that Hank left behind.

2. Pearl with Drew, *Minnie Pearl,* 210.

3. John W. Rumble works out the complications of the relationship in "Fred Rose," 90–93.

4. Guralnick, *Lost Highway,* 211.

5. Nick Tosches is good on this subject in *Country,* 31ff.

6. Shelton, *The Country Music Story,* 91.

7. Horstman, *Sing Your Heart out,* 137.

8. Ibid., 139.

9. L. Williams with Rankin, *Our Hank Williams.*

10. Tosches, *Country*, 24.

11. Guralnick, *Lost Highway*, 98.

12. Wilmeth, "Southern Regionalism," 250–55.

13. Pearl with Drew, *Minnie Pearl*, 215.

14. Carter, "Hank Williams's Ghost," 29.

15. Blount, *Crackers*, 190.

Chapter 3

1. Wilmeth, "Textual Problems," 379–406.

2. Rankin, "Rankin File," 4 April 1948, 3B.

3. Rankin, "Rankin File," 4 February 1953.

4. R. M. Williams, *Sing a Sad Song*, 184.

5. The interview is reprinted in Moore, *Hank Williams*, 48. It appeared originally in the June 1953 issue of *Country Song Roundup*, 12.

6. Rivers, *Hank Williams*, 22.

7. Shestack, "Hank Williams," 301–6. The interview is reprinted in "Hank Williams: He Had Country Soul," in *The Songs of Hank Williams*, 7–26.

8. Gleason, "Perspectives," 32.

9. Jarman, "Country Music Goes to Town," 49. The interview is reprinted in Gentry, *A History and Encyclopedia*, 115–24.

CHRONOLOGY

1891   22 December, birth of Elonzo Huble Williams, father of Hank Williams, in Lowndes County, Alabama, near the small town of Braggs.

1897   24 August, birth of Fred Rose in Evansville, Illinois.

1898   12 August, birth of Jessie Lillie Belle Skipper, mother of Hank Williams, in Butler County, Alabama.

1916   12 November, marriage of Jessie Lillie Belle Skipper and Elonzo Huble Williams.

1922   8 August, birth of Irene Williams, Hank's older sister, to Lillie and Lon Williams in Mount Olive Community, Alabama.

1923   28 February, birth of Audrey Mae Sheppard, Hank's first wife, in Pike County, Alabama; 17 September, birth of Hiram "Hank" Williams to Lillie and Lon Williams in Mount Olive Community, Alabama.

1925   28 November, beginning of the WSM ("We Shield Millions") Barn Dance, sponsored by National Life and Accident Insurance Company, in Nashville. The Barn Dance became The Grand Ole Opry in 1927.

1929   November, Lon Williams entered the Veterans Administration Hospital in Biloxi, Mississippi.

1930   The family moved to Georgiana, Alabama, where Lillie ran a boarding-house. Hank may have met Rufe "Tee Tot" Payne here.

1934–5   Hank spent the school year with his relatives, the McNeils, at the Pool lumber camp near Fountain in Monroe County, Alabama.

1935   The Williams family moved to Greenville, Alabama.

1937   July, the Williams family moved to Montgomery. That fall, Hank won the Empire Theatre talent contest, singing his own composition, "The WPA Blues." He began making appearances on radio station WSFA.

1941   13 August, birth of Lycrecia Ann Guy to Audrey Sheppard Guy and James Erskine Guy in Pike County, Alabama.

1942   12 September, Lon Williams, now divorced from Lillie, married Ola Till in McWilliams, Alabama; Fred Rose and Roy Acuff established Acuff-Rose Publishing Company. Hank probably met Audrey Sheppard Guy in this year. After being rejected by the Selective Service because of his back, the nineteen-year-old Hank dropped out of the ninth grade and went to Mobile, where he took a job with the Alabama Drydock and Shipbuilding Company.

1943   19 June, birth of Hank's half-sister, Leila Williams, to Lon and Ola Williams.

1944   Fall, Hank returned to Montgomery from Mobile; 5 December, Audrey divorced Erskine Guy. The decree stipulated a sixty-day reconciliation period before either could remarry; 15 December, Audrey and Hank were married in a Texaco service station near Andalusia, Alabama. The wedding took place fifty days before Audrey's reconciliation period with Erskine Guy had expired.

1944–5   Hank was a regular on WSFA and was touring the area with the Drifting Cowboys. He published his first songbook, *Songs of Hank Williams, "The Drifting Cowboy,"* which included ten songs.

1945   Hank's first hospitalization for alcoholism, in Prattville, Alabama.

1946   14 September, Hank and Audrey traveled to Nashville to meet Fred and Wesley Rose; 11 December, Hank's first recording session, at WSM Studio D, Castle Recording Company. He cut four of his own songs for Sterling: "Calling You," "Never Again (Will I Knock on Your Door)," "Wealth Won't Save Your Soul," and "When God Comes and Gathers His Jewels;" Hank published his second song book, *Hank Williams and His Drifting Cowboys, Stars of WSFA, Deluxe Song Book,* which included thirty songs.

1947   21 April, Nashville recording session that included "Move It on Over" and "I Saw the Light." This was Hank's first session for MGM and Frank Walker; 6 November, Nashville recording session that included the best known version of "Honky Tonkin'."

1948   3 April, opening of the Louisiana Hayride in Shreveport; 26 May, Audrey divorced Hank for the first time, in Montgomery; August, Hank became a regular on the Louisiana Hayride; 22 December, Cincinnati recording session that included "Lovesick Blues."

1949 25 February, MGM released "Lovesick Blues," which was to become *Billboard*'s number one hit of the year. It was on the charts for forty-two weeks and undoubtedly helped get Hank onto The Grand Ole Opry; 26 May, Randall Hank Williams, "Hank Jr.," was born in Shreveport, Louisiana; 11 June, Hank made his debut on The Grand Ole Opry, singing "Lovesick Blues;" August, Hank and Audrey purchased their home at 4916 Franklin Road in Nashville; 9 August, The divorce of 26 May 1948 was amended *nunc pro tunc*; 30 August, Recording session in Cincinnati that included "I'm So Lonesome I Could Cry" and "My Bucket's Got a Hole in It;" Fall, Hank's first trip to "The Hut," Madison Sanitarium, in Nashville; October, Hank recorded eight radio shows on 16-inch records for the LeBlanc Corporation; 13 November, Hank and Audrey began a tour of Armed Forces bases in Germany with Red Foley, Roy Acuff, Minnie Pearl, Jimmy Dickens, and others. The tour ended on Thanksgiving.

1950 9 January, Nashville recording session that included "Long Gone Lonesome Blues" and "Why Don't You Love Me?" This was the first session with the Drifting Cowboys; 10 January, Nashville recording session that included Hank's first two cuts under the pseudonym "Luke the Drifter;" 21 December, Nashville recording session that included "Cold, Cold Heart;" Hank had three songs on *Billboard*'s yearly retail sales chart: "Why Don't You Love Me" (4), "Long Gone Lonesome Blues" (5), and "Moanin' the Blues" (30).

1951 16 March, Nashville recording session that included "I Can't Help It (If I'm Still in Love with You)" and "Hey Good Lookin'"; 23 March, Hank and Audrey recorded "The Pale Horse and His Rider" and "A Home in Heaven"; 21 May, Hank was admitted to the North Louisiana Sanitarium in Shreveport to be treated for his alcoholism and his back problem. He was released on 24 May; 10 August, Nashville recording session that included "Half as Much;" 15 August, The Hadacol Caravan began in New Iberia, Louisiana. The tour was supposed to run until 2 October, but it ended after thirty-four shows on 18 September in Dallas; 24 September, The *Nashville Banner* announced that Hank had signed a movie contract with MGM. Hank was never to be involved in the production of a movie, however; 13 December, Hank had back surgery at the Vanderbilt University Hospital. He was released on 24 December; Nashville's Harpeth Publishing produced *How to Write Folk and Western Music to Sell,* by Hank and Jimmy Rule. Hank and Audrey's Corral, a western wear store, opened on Commerce Street in Nashville. Hank had three songs on *Billboard*'s yearly retail sales chart: "Cold, Cold Heart" (1), "Hey Good Lookin'" (8), and "Crazy Heart" (29).

1952   3 January, Hank moved out of the Franklin Road home. A week later, Audrey filed for separate maintenance; 29 May, The divorce of Hank and Audrey Williams was completed; 13 June, Recording session in Nashville that included "Jambalaya," "Settin' the Woods on Fire," and "I'll Never Get out of This World Alive;" Summer, Hank met Billie Jean Jones Eshliman, who had recently moved to Nashville from Bossier City, Louisiana; 11 July, Nashville recording session that included "You Win Again;" 11 August, Jim Denny fired Hank from The Grand Ole Opry. "Jambalaya" was on its way to being the number one song at the time. Hank went home to Montgomery; 15 August, Hank and disc jockey Bob McKinnon went to Lake Martin, not too far from Montgomery and near the Creek Indian town called Kowaliga, the inspiration of the title "Kaw-Liga;" 17 August, Hank was arrested in Alexander City, Alabama for being drunk and disorderly; 20 September, Hank appeared on the Louisiana Hayride; 23 September, Hank's last commercial recording session, in Nashville. He cut "I Could Never Be Ashamed of You," "Your Cheatin' Heart," "Kaw-Liga," and "Take These Chains from My Heart." That last song would be the number one hit for four weeks; 15 October, Hank and Bobbie Jett executed their contract regarding their unborn child; 18 October, Hank married Billie Jean Jones Eshliman in Minden, Louisiana. The next day they married again, once at a matinee and then at an evening performance at the New Orleans Civic Auditorium; 28 October, Billie Jean's divorce from Harrison Holland Eshliman became final; 31 October, Hank was admitted to the North Louisiana Sanitarium. He returned to the sanitarium on 27 November and on 11 December 1952; 21 December, Hank and Billie Jean visited Taft and Erleen Skipper in Georgiana. The next day, Hank sang "The Log Train" at Taft's store; 28 December, Hank performed for the Montgomery chapter of the American Federation of Musicians; 30 December, Hank left Montgomery for a New Year's Day show in Canton, Ohio; Hank had three songs on *Billboard*'s yearly retail sales chart: "Jambalaya" (3),"Half as Much" (11), and "Honky Tonk Blues" (28).

1953   1 January, Hank was dead on arrival at the Oak Hill Hospital in Oak Hill, West Virginia. "Jambalaya" was *Billboard*'s number one song at that moment; 4 January, Hank's funeral was held at the Montgomery City Auditorium. He was buried later that day in the Oakwood Cemetery Annex. His body was moved to its present grave in the cemetery on 17 January 1953; 6 January, Antha Belle Jett, daughter of Bobbie Jett and Hank Williams, was born; Billie Jean Jones Williams forfeited all claims to the name and estate of Hank Williams for $30,000. Hank had three songs on *Billboard*'s yearly retail sales chart: "Kaw-Liga" (1), "Your Cheatin' Heart" (2), and "Take These Chains from My Heart" (9).

1954   21 September, Hank's tombstone was unveiled in Montgomery; 1 December, Fred Rose died; 23 December, Lillie completed the adoption of Antha Belle Jett, changing the child's name to Cathy Yvone Stone; Billie Jean married Johnny Horton, who died in an automobile accident on 5 November 1960.

1955   26 February, Lillie died in her sleep. She was buried to Hank's immediate left. About a month later, Cathy Stone became a ward of the state of Alabama and was put into a licensed foster home.

1959   23 April, Cathy Stone was adopted by Wayne and Louise Deupree, who changed the child's name to Cathy Louise Deupree.

1961   Hank Williams, Jimmie Rodgers, and Fred Rose became the first members of the Country Music Hall of Fame.

1964   4 November, The MGM movie, *Your Cheatin' Heart*, premiered at the Paramount Theatre in Montgomery.

1970   23 October, Elonzo Huble Williams, Hank's father, died; Roger Williams published *Sing a Sad Song: The Life of Hank Williams*, the first scholarly treatment of the star.

1972   12 December, Shelton Hank Williams (Hank Williams III) was born to Hank Jr. and his second wife, Gwendolyn Sue Yeargin.

1975   22 October, U.S. District Judge L. Clure Morton ruled in Nashville that Billie Jean had been Hank's wife at the time of his death and that she should share in the copyright renewals; 4 November, Audrey Williams died. She was buried in the Oakwood Cemetery Annex, but at some distance from Hank. In 1983, Hank Jr. and Lycrecia had her grave moved to a spot beside Hank's.

1981   Time/Life inaugurated its Country and Western Classics series with an issue on Hank Williams.

1985   Cathy Louise Deupree began her long litigation for part of the Williams estate. In 1993, she was awarded a share of the Williams publishing and royalty legacy. She changed her name to Jett Williams.

1995   23 March, Irene Williams Smith died.

1998   September, Mercury released "The Complete Hank Williams," the definitive ten-compact-disc set of Hank's recordings.

BIBLIOGRAPHY

Agee, James, and Walker Evans. *Let Us Now Praise Famous Men.* Boston: Houghton Mifflin, 1941.

Arp, Jim. *The First Outlaw: Hank Williams.* Kings Mountain, N.C.: A & B Enterprises, 1949.

Bane, Michael. *White Boy Singin' the Blues: The Black Roots of White Rock.* New York: Penguin, 1982.

Beifuss, John. "Onetime Hank Williams Sidewoman Still Keeps a 'Solid Beat'." *The Commercial Appeal (Memphis),* 15 September 2000, F1.

The Best of Hank Williams. Milwaukee, Wis.: Hal Leonard Publishing, 1982.

Blount, Roy. *Crackers.* New York: Knopf, 1980.

Bock, Al. *I Saw the Light: The Gospel Life of Hank Williams.* Nashville, Tenn.: Green Valley Record Store, 1979.

Campbell, Roy. "Little Skeeter's Gotta Learn." *Hustler,* March 1978, 68–90.

Caress, Jay. *Hank Williams: Country Music's Tragic King.* New York: Stein and Day, 1979.

Carter, Walter. "Hank Williams's Ghost Blacks out Opry House." *The Tennessean,* 28 July 1982, 29.

Clay, Floyd Martin. *Couzain Dudley LeBlanc: From Huey Long to Hadacol.* Gretna, La.: Pelican Publishing, 1973.

Clayton, Frank. "Remembering Hank." *Alabama Journal,* 20 February 1971, 4.

The Complete Works of Hank Williams: A 129 Song Legacy of His Music. New York: Acuff-Rose International, 1980.

Country Music Magazine, 3 (March 1975).

Country Song Roundup, 1 (June 1953).

"Court to Air Late Singer's Marital Status." *Atlanta Journal*, 23 October 1969, 2A.

Cusic, Don, ed. *Hank Williams: The Complete Lyrics*. New York: St. Martin's Press, 1993.

"Damages Denied to Williams' Widow." *Atlanta Journal*, 6 March 1972, 2A.

Deal, Babs H. *High Lonesome World: The Death and Life of a Country Music Singer*. New York: Doubleday, 1969.

Escott, Colin, with Martin Hawkins. *Good Rockin' Tonight: Sun Records and the Birth of Rock 'n Roll*. New York: St. Martin's Press, 1991.

Escott, Colin, with George Merritt and William MacEwen. *Hank Williams: The Biography*. Boston: Little, Brown, 1994.

E-Z Way Edition [of Hank Williams's Music]. Milwaukee, Wis.: Hal Leonard Publishing, 1982.

Flippo, Chet. "Hank Williams Hits the Opry: 1949." *The Journal of Country Music*, 8, no. 3 (undated), 5–17.

Flippo, Chet. *Your Cheatin' Heart: A Biography of Hank Williams*. New York: Simon and Schuster, 1981.

Friedman, Kinky. *A Case of Lone Star*. New York: William Morrow, 1987.

Friedman, Kinky. *Roadkill*. New York: Simon and Schuster, 1997.

Gentry, Linnell, ed.. *A History and Encyclopedia of Country, Western, and Gospel Music*. St. Claire Shores, Mich.: Scholarly Press, 1972.

Gilbert, Elizabeth. "The Ghost." *GQ*, December 2000, 304–11, 346–9.

Gleason, Ralph J. "Perspectives: Hank Williams, Roy Acuff and Then God!!" *Rolling Stone*, 28 June 1969, 32.

Graves, John Temple, II, ed. *The Book of Alabama and the South*. Birmingham, Ala.: The Protective Life Insurance Company, 1933.

Guralnick, Peter. *Lost Highway: Journeys and Arrivals of American Musicians*. Boston: David R. Godine, 1979. Reprint, Boston: Little, Brown, 1999.

Halberstam, David. "Hank Williams Remembered." *Look*, 35 (13 July 1971), 42.

Hank as We Knew Him: Memories of the Early Life of Hank Williams as Recalled by Some of Those Who Knew Him. Georgiana and Chapman, Ala.: The Three Arts Club of Georgiana and Chapman, 1982.

"Hank's Widow Illegally Wed." *Alabama Journal*, 15 January 1953, 1A, 7A.

Hank Williams and His Drifting Cowboys, Stars of WSFA, Deluxe Song Book. Montgomery, Ala.: WSFA, circa 1946.

Hank Williams' Country Hit Parade. Nashville, Tenn.: Fred Rose Music, circa 1951.

Hank Williams' Country Music Folio. Nashville, Tenn.: Fred Rose Music, circa 1952.

Hank Williams Family Photo Album No. 1. Nashville, Tenn.: The Hank Williams Memorial Foundation, undated.

Hank Williams Family Photo Album No. 2. Nashville, Tenn.: The Hank Williams Memorial Foundation, undated.

Hank Williams' Favorite Songs. Nashville, Tenn.: Fred Rose Music, 1953.

"Hank Williams Immortal to Cornball Fans." *Variety,* 190 (29 April 1953), 10, 52.

Hank Williams Memorial Souvenir Program. Montgomery, Ala.: The Alcazar Temple, 1954.

Hank Williams: The Complete Works: A 128 Song Legacy of His Music. New York: Warner Brothers, 1999.

"Heart Condition Killed Hank, Coroner's Jury Says in Report." *Montgomery Advertiser,* 11 January 1953, 1A, 8A.

Hemphill, Paul. *The Nashville Sound: Bright Lights and Country Music.* New York: Simon and Schuster, 1970.

Horstman, Dorothy. *Sing Your Heart out, Country Boy.* New York: Dutton, 1975.

Hurst, Jack. *Nashville's Grand Ole Opry.* New York: Harry R. Abrams, 1975.

Jarman, Rufus. "Country Music Goes to Town." *Nation's Business,* 41 (February 1953), 44–9. Reprinted in *A History and Encyclopedia of Country, Western, and Gospel Music,* edited by Linnell Gentry, 115–24. St. Claire Shores, Mich.: Scholarly Press, 1972.

Johnson, Rheta G. "Hank's Hold on Hometown Grows Stronger." *Atlanta Journal-Constitution,* 5 March 1999, D2.

Kane, Hartnett T. *Louisiana Hayride: The American Rehearsal for Dictatorship, 1928–1940.* New York: William Morrow, 1941.

King, Larry. "The 'Hillbilly Shakespeare' Left 'Em Sobbing in Their Beer." *TV Guide,* 5 March 1983, 42–5.

Koon, George William. *Hank Williams: A Bio-bibliography.* Westport, Conn.: Greenwood Press, 1983.

Krishef, Robert K. *Hank Williams.* Minneapolis, Minn.: Lerner Publications, 1978.

Leppert, Richard, and George Lipsitz. "Age, the Body, and Experience in the Music of Hank Williams." *Popular Music,* I (1990), 259–74.

Lindeman, Edith. "Hank Williams Hillbilly Show Is Different: Star Makes Impression of an Unexpected Kind." *The Richmond Times-Dispatch,* 30 January 1952, 18.

Linn, Ed. "The Short Life of Hank Williams." *Saga,* January 1957, 8–11, 86–91.

Logan, Horace, with Bill Sloan. *Elvis, Hank, and Me: Making Musical History on the Louisiana Hayride.* New York: St. Martin's, 1998.

Longino, Miriam. "Legacy of Hank." *Atlanta Journal-Constitution*, 20 September 1998, L1, L5.

Longino, Miriam. "Singer Left Behind a Smoldering Family Feud." *Atlanta Journal-Constitution*, 20 September 1998, L5.

Malone, Bill C. *Country Music U.S.A.: A Fifty-Year History*. Austin: University of Texas Press, 1968.

Malone, Bill C. *Singing Cowboys and Musical Mountaineers: Southern Culture and the Roots of Country Music*. Athens: University of Georgia Press, 1993.

Malone, Bill C., and Judith McCulloh, eds. *Stars of Country Music: Uncle Dave Macon to Johnny Rodriguez*. Urbana: University of Illinois Press, 1975.

Mankelow, David. "Legend." *Country*, 2 (April 1973), 30–2.

McKee, Charles B. Hank Williams scrapbook. Montgomery: Alabama Department of Archives and History.

Montgomery Advertiser—Alabama Journal, 11 January 1953.

Moore, Thurston, ed. *Hank Williams, the Legend*. Denver, Colo.: Heather Enterprises, 1972.

Morris, Doug. "Hank Williams' Death Still Issue." *The Knoxville Journal*, 15 December 1982, C1.

Mortland, John. "Hank Williams." *Creem*, April 1973, 68–9.

Odom, Mr. and Mrs. Burton. *The Hank Williams Story*. Butler County, Ala.: The Butler County Historical Association, 1974.

"Oklahoma Committee Told Phony Physician Prescribed Sedative for Hank Williams." *Montgomery Advertiser*, 12 March 1953, 10A.

Pearl, Minnie, with Joan Drew. *Minnie Pearl: An Autobiography*. New York: Simon and Schuster, 1980.

Piazza, Tom. "Still Standing Tall over Country." *The New York Times*, 8 November 1998, 36, 41.

Pleasants, Henry E. *The Great American Popular Singers*. New York: Simon and Schuster, 1974.

Porterfield, Nolan. *Jimmie Rodgers: The Life and Times of America's Blue Yodeler*. Urbana: University of Illinois Press, 1979.

Pruden, Wesley. "Ol' Hank: 'Widow Williams' Settles Old Score." *The National Observer*, 12 July 1971, 1, 14.

Rankin, Allen. "Rankin File." *Montgomery Advertiser*, 4 April 1948, 3B.

Rankin, Allen. "Rankin File." *Montgomery Advertiser*, 29 December 1952, no pagination.

Rankin, Allen. "Rankin File." *Montgomery Advertiser*, 4 February 1953, no pagination.

Rivers, Jerry. *Hank Williams: From Life to Legend.* Denver, Colo.: Heather Enterprises, 1967. Rivers reissued the book from his home in Goodlettsville, Tenn., ca. 1981.

Rockwell, Harry E. *Beneath the Applause: A Story about Country and Western Music Written by a Fan.* Published privately by Rockwell, 1973.

Rumble, John W. "Fred Rose and the Development of the Nashville Music Industry, 1942–1954." Ph.D. diss., Vanderbilt University, 1980.

"Sadly the Troubadour." *Newsweek,* 41 (19 January 1953), 55.

Shelton, Robert, with photos by Burt Goldblatt. *The Country Music Story: A Picture History of Country and Western Music.* New York: Bobbs-Merrill, 1966.

Shestack, Melvin. "Hank Williams." In *The Country Music Encyclopedia,* 301–306. New York: Thomas Y. Crowell, 1974.

Shestack, Melvin. "The World's Not Yet Lonesome for Me." *Country Music,* 1 (January 1973), 38–46.

Songs from Your Cheatin' Heart. Nashville, Tenn.: Fred Rose Music and Milene Music, circa 1964.

The Songs of Hank Williams. New York: Acuff-Rose International, circa 1975.

Songs of Hank Williams, "The Drifting Cowboy." Montgomery, Ala.: WSFA, circa 1945.

Tosches, Nick. *Country: The Biggest Music in America.* New York: Stein and Day, 1977.

Waldron, Eli. "The Death of Hank Williams." *The Reporter,* 12 (19 May 1955), 35–7.

Waldron, Eli. "The Life and Death of a Country Singer." *Coronet,* 39 (January 1956), 40–5.

"Widow of Singer Loses Second Suit." *Atlanta Journal,* 1 August 1972, 9B.

Williams, Hank, and Jimmy Rule. *How to Write Folk and Western Music to Sell.* Nashville, Tenn.: Harpeth Publishing, 1951.

Williams, Hank, Jr., with Michael Bane. *Living Proof.* New York: G. P. Putnam's Sons, 1979.

Williams, Jett, with Pamela Thomas. *Ain't Nothin' as Sweet as My Baby: The Story of Hank Williams' Lost Daughter.* New York: Harcourt Brace Jovanovich, 1990.

Williams, Lillie, with Allen Rankin. *Our Hank Williams: "The Drifting Cowboy."* Montgomery, Ala.: Philbert Publications, 1953. The basic materials of this book first appeared in *Montgomery Advertiser—Alabama Journal,* 11 January 1953, no pagination.

Williams, Lycrecia, with Dale Vinicur. *Still in Love with You: The Story of Hank and Audrey Williams.* Nashville, Tenn.: Rutledge Hill Press, 1989.

Williams, Roger M. "Hank Williams." In *Stars of Country Music: Uncle Dave Macon to Johnny Rodriguez*, edited by Bill C. Malone and Judith McCulloh, 237–54. Urbana: University of Illinois Press, 1975.

Williams, Roger M. *Hank Williams*. With notes on the music by Charles K. Wolfe and Bob Pinson. Alexandria, Va.: Time/Life Books, 1981.

Williams, Roger M. *Sing a Sad Song: The Life of Hank Williams*. New York: Doubleday, 1970. Reprint, New York: Ballantine Books, 1973.

Williams, Roger M. *Sing a Sad Song: The Life of Hank Williams*. 2d ed., with discography by Bob Pinson. Urbana: University of Illinois Press, 1981.

Williams, Roger M. "Writing about Hank." *Country Music*, 1 (May 1973), 58–61.

"Williams' Widow Again Sues MGM." *Atlanta Journal*, 4 May 1972, 4B.

"Williams' Widow Loses Suit." *Atlanta Constitution*, 2 August 1972, 13A.

Wilmeth, Thomas L. "'Pictures from Life's Other Side': Southern Regionalism in Hank Williams's Luke the Drifter Recordings." In *Language Variety in the South Revisited*, edited by Cynthia Bernstein, Thomas Nunnally, and Robin Sabino, 250–55. Tuscaloosa: University of Alabama Press, 1997.

Wilmeth, Thomas L. "Textual Problems with the Canon of Hank Williams." *Papers of the Bibliographical Society of America*, 93 (September 1999), 379–406.

Wolfe, Charles K. *Tennessee Strings: The Story of Country Music in Tennessee*. Knoxville: University of Tennessee Press, 1977.

INDEX

References to figures appear in *italics*.